Ignorance Is No Defense®
A College Student's Guide to North Carolina Law

2010 Edition

J.Tom Morgan
and
Wilson Parker

Ignorance Is No Defense®
A College Student's Guide to North Carolina Law
2010 Edition

J.Tom Morgan
and
Wilson Parker

Published by Westchester Legal Press, LLC

Decatur, GA

ISBN: 978-0-9819397-3-5

Library of Congress Cataloging-in-Publication Data available upon request

©2010 Westchester Legal Press, LLC

If you have questions or comments about this book, please contact the authors by e-mailing info@ignoranceisnodefense.com or finding us on Facebook.

www.ignoranceisnodefense.com

Design and layout by Allison Schwartz (www.allison-schwartz.com)

This book is dedicated to
Carol Ellis Morgan
for her wisdom, grace, and love.

To Order This Book

Online

Purchase at www.ignoranceisnodefense.com or www.amazon.com

Purchase Orders

Send or FAX your purchase order to:

Westchester Legal Press, LLC
P.O. Box 1324
Decatur, GA 30031

E-mail: info@ignoranceisnodefense.com

FAX: (404) 373-6418

Phone

Call: (404) 373-6453

For Speaking Engagements

Contact J.Tom Morgan or Wilson Parker at
info@ignoranceisnodefense.com

www.ignoranceisnodefense.com

Acknowledgments

The authors would like to thank the following people for their contributions to this project – first and foremost, Susan Sullivan, Wake Forest Law School Class of 2011, for her meticulous organization, superb research, and unfailing good humor; Larry Southerland, for his relentless pursuit of accuracy in substance and style and his unceasing acts of friendship; the Honorable Stuart Albright, the Honorable Lawrence Fine, and Stephanie Reese, for providing invaluable insights into the real world of North Carolina's court system; Fountain Walker, former chief of police at Davidson College, for his incomparable guidance during the development of this book; Charlene Cerutti, Harold Holmes, Regina Lawson, Dina Marty, Marianne Schubert, and Ken Zick, for offering thoughtful perspectives regarding issues confronting students and administrators on college campuses; Logan Smalley, John Petrey, and Peter McDonald, for their ideas and enthusiastic support for this book; Carol Sowell, for her unsurpassed administrative skills; and Mrs. Ann Wooten, for her tireless work on behalf of North Carolina students and for providing the impetus to take the information in this book to college campuses. Finally, our deep gratitude and appreciation for the talented and indefatigable loved ones whose long hours and diligent work made this truly a family effort: our fearless editor-in-chief, Carol Ellis Morgan; our project manager extraordinaire, Caroline Morgan; and our tenacious and gifted editorial assistants, John Morgan, Laurel Simmons, and Brandon Simmons. Because of all of you, we are able, honored, and proud to publish this book.

Reviews

Praise for *Ignorance Is No Defense,*
A Teenager's Guide to Georgia Law
by J. Tom Morgan

"J. Tom Morgan, using his expertise as both a prosecutor and a defense lawyer, explains the law in a manner that is both readable and informative and uses real-life examples that are relevant for teenagers."
> **-Judge Martha K. Glaze**, Retired Juvenile Court Judge, Clayton County, GA

"A must-read for every Georgia teenager and parent."
> **-Susan Hoffman**, GPTV

"With J. Tom Morgan's clear and comprehensive guide, teenagers can readily access information to help them make wise choices and avoid being on the other side of the law. Every Georgia teenager needs a copy of this book."
> **-Kenneth B. Hodges III**, Former District Attorney, Dougherty Judicial Circuit, GA

"J. Tom Morgan captured the attention of students and parents with hard-hitting and relevant information on Georgia laws that can make a marked impact on a teen's life. Mr. Morgan's book is a must-read for teenagers and their parents."
> **-Linda Cooper**, PTSO Co-President 2007-2009, Dunwoody High School

"Every child in Georgia needs a copy of that book!"
> **-Marlene Melvin**, Curriculum and Activities Director, State Bar of Georgia

"Should be on every book club list. This book should be required reading for every Georgia high school student."
> **-Linda Wright**, Member, Board of Education, Gilmer County

Did You Know . . . ?

? Did You Know that if a police officer asks permission to search you, your pockets, your car, your book bag, or anything else that belongs to you, you always have the right to refuse to consent to the search? *See Chapter Six, Your Constitutional Rights: Search and Seizure.*

? Did You Know that giving a prescription drug to a friend may be a felony? *See Chapter Eleven, Possession and Sale of Legal and Illegal Drugs.*

? Did You Know that conviction for purchase, possession, or consumption of alcohol by a person under 21 years old - or conviction for furnishing alcohol to a person under 21 years old - can result in a 1-year revocation of your driver's license? *See Chapter Nine, Alcohol and Underage Drinking.*

? Did You Know that you commit rape if you have sex with someone who is too intoxicated to give consent? *See Chapter Fifteen, Sex Crimes with Force.*

Ignorance Is No Defense,
A College Student's Guide to North Carolina Law
addresses these questions and more.

Table of Contents

VI. Safety and Injury: Threats and Bodily Harm to You and Others

VII. Property: Your Property and the Property of Others

VIII. Staying the Course: Driving, Driving Violations, and Accidents

IX. Other Criminal Laws and Topics of Interest: Groups and Group Initiations, Crimes Against Children, and More

X. Landlord/Tenant

Introduction and Guide to Reading

Introduction

The rights and responsibilities for college students under the laws of the State of North Carolina are the same as they are for adults. The college environment, though, can provide more access and opportunity to break the law than students may have experienced at home. For most college students, the move to college is the first move away from home. With expanded freedom comes greater responsibility, as well as more opportunities to make decisions about legal and illegal behavior. Students are not always informed about the local laws and the consequences of violating them, or their rights and responsibilities under these laws. Many students attending North Carolina colleges are not residents of this state and may not realize how the laws and punishments differ from their home states. Students may not be aware that college employees and administrators also have certain rights.

This book will enable North Carolina college students to make informed decisions. The book covers legal topics relevant to college students. Criminal laws discussed include underage drinking, fake IDs, possession of drugs, driving under the influence, theft, vandalism, sex crimes (such as date rape), and assault. Additionally, the book explains a student's Constitutional rights on a college campus. Some civil law topics, such as landlord/tenant and social host laws, are also discussed.

Unfortunately, students also find themselves in situations where they are victims of crimes. Sometimes students do not even realize that they are victims. This book will help students recognize these situations and understand their rights.

The purpose of this book is to empower young adults with knowledge about North Carolina laws that affect them, to enable early intervention in problem situations, and to prevent problems from arising in the first place. The ultimate goal is for students to lead safe, happy, and fulfilling lives in college – engaging their questioning minds and fun-loving spirits – without encountering the criminal justice system.

College Students and the Law

College students are often unaware of the legal consequences of their actions, both on and off campus. With most crimes, whether or not you intend to commit a *crime* is simply not relevant. The only thing that is important is whether or not you intend to commit the *act* that results in a crime. Students will not be able to defend themselves by saying it was only an accident or joke or that they didn't know they were committing a crime. Many people do not realize the long-term and wide-ranging effects of a criminal conviction – even a misdemeanor conviction – on their criminal history. For instance, a criminal conviction can adversely affect job applications, graduate school applications, eligibility for student loans, driver's license privileges, and automobile insurance rates.

Campus Law and Common Practice

Colleges handle legal infractions in different ways. For example, college administrators may choose to deal with matters internally without reporting the crimes to the state (*i.e.*, without calling outside police to make an arrest or to deliver a citation). Students may have the illusion that because some incidents are dealt with through college administration, the actions of students are not subject to legal recourse. While college administrators have some discretion over whether they report an on-campus incident to the state, the bottom line is this: if the law is broken in the state of North Carolina, even if the crime occurs on a college campus, the offenders may be subject to the state judicial system and the consequences of a state prosecution in addition to the policies of their colleges.

Our Responsibility and Our Inspiration

Because "ignorance is no defense" to a violation of law, our legal profession has a duty to ensure that students, parents, and educators are informed about the law. With proper education and understanding, we have found that college students usually respect and follow the laws.

Our inspiration for the book comes from working with students and young adults over the course of our professional careers. Wilson is a professor of Constitutional Law at Wake Forest University

School of Law and is licensed to practice law in both North Carolina and Georgia. J.Tom is a former District Attorney, is currently a lawyer in private practice in DeKalb County, Georgia, and is licensed to practice law in both North Carolina and Georgia. J.Tom is also an adjunct professor at Georgia State University College of Law. Combined, they have prosecuted, defended, counseled, educated, and spoken to thousands of young adults during their careers. Also, and maybe most importantly, they have raised five college students of their own, four of whom attended colleges in North Carolina.

Guide to Reading

This book describes laws in North Carolina that may affect college students. We compiled the laws based on 1) our experiences as attorneys in the public and private sector, and 2) our experiences as educators. Many of the examples used in the book involve actual cases and are representative of realistic events on North Carolina college campuses.

To protect the privacy of individuals, we have not used real names. Sometimes, we use "**P**" or "**V**" in examples. **P** refers to the perpetrator of the crime, and **V** refers to the victim of the crime, if the example includes a victim.

Most of the laws described in the book are criminal laws. We also discuss some non-criminal laws, such as landlord/tenant and social host laws.

Sections divide the book into common, related subjects (for example, *Substances*). **Chapters** discuss the laws surrounding specific topics in the section (for example, *Alcohol and Underage Drinking* is a chapter in the *Substances* section). The **Glossary** defines terms you need to know. The **Index** helps you quickly find where a law or subject is discussed in the text. If you want to read the North Carolina statute relating to one of the subjects in this book, the **Appendix** provides a list of citations. The **Appendix** also lists several useful websites.

Our job is to present the laws so that readers easily understand the laws and the consequences of violating them. We do not express any opinions as to the virtue or wisdom of any of the laws mentioned in this book.

The purpose of our book is to be a helpful guide to North Carolina college students and young adults. The book is not intended to be a comprehensive treatise on North Carolina's criminal and civil laws. It is a general reference. Our book is not intended to give legal advice to someone who may be in trouble with the law. Your particular facts and circumstances may be different from situations described in the book. In addition, many police departments and district attorney offices have very different approaches to the enforcement and prosecution of the same statutes. Purchasing this book does not establish an attorney-client relationship. If you find yourself in trouble, you need to consult an attorney who is familiar with the legal environment in your community. Finally, while we make every effort to update this book on our website, laws change over time. The specifics of any statute mentioned in this book must be checked for its precise wording as of the time that it might apply to you. Ordinarily, you would need an attorney to assist you to do that. Citations for the statutes are in the Appendix.

We hope you enjoy this book. Please contact us with your questions and comments by visiting our website – **www.ignoranceisnodefense.com/nc** – or finding us on Facebook®. We look forward to hearing from you.

I. Starting College

Chapter 1
Welcome to College

Chapter 1
Welcome to College

Under North Carolina law, turning 18 years old brings new rights and responsibilities. Most importantly, you are legally an adult, and you are no longer considered a minor under the control of your parents. This new status is particularly relevant to your new relationship with the college or university you are attending. While in high school, you were under the authority of your parents, and the high school was given similar broad discretion in its relationship with you.

Now, at 18, you have the legal authority to sign binding contracts. You are at your college or university because you have elected to be there. Essentially, you have a contractual relationship with your college. Your college sets out in contracts – *e.g.*, enrollment agreements, housing agreements, codes of conduct, etc. – the expectations that it requires of its students. Failure to meet these expectations is a violation of the terms of the contract. The consequences of such a failure will be outlined in the contract – possibly suspension or expulsion. In addition, while in high school, you were involved in a three-way relationship: between you, your school, and your parents. In college (with a few exceptions we will note later), only you are involved with your school.

The (non-existent) College Bubble

Your experiences at college enable you to grow from an adolescent into a young adult, progressing intellectually, socially, and emotionally. College professionals don't enter academia to spend their time disciplining students. However, they have an obligation to the community to do all they can to ensure that your college experience is safe – that you are neither harmed nor allowed to harm another.

Many students are under the illusion that colleges exist in a "bubble." They think that the rules that apply in the outside world don't apply on campus, and conversely, that anything they do in the outside world is irrelevant to their status as students. This is a variation of the misconception that "what happens in Vegas stays in Vegas" (when, in fact, what happens in Vegas stays on Facebook®). In reality, the laws of the State of North Carolina apply everywhere in North Carolina. There is no "free zone" on a college campus.

You and Your College: A Legal, Contractual, and Moral Relationship

It is useful to think about your new status as a college student as one that is governed legally, contractually, and morally. These three distinct standards involve: 1) the laws of the State of North Carolina; 2) the contracts you signed with your college; and 3) the morals of your new college community.

Legal Obligations

The criminal laws of North Carolina are particularly relevant to college students. If you violate the criminal law, you are subject to prosecution by the State of North Carolina. We address the laws that college students are most likely to confront in detail throughout the rest of the book. In addition, students 18 and over, like all other adults, are also held responsible for civil liability if their behavior harms another – even if it does not violate a criminal law. This involves "being sued," whether for injuring someone (*e.g.,* a car wreck) or for breaking a contract (*e.g.,* a lease). We address this topic later in the book.

Police and Law Enforcement

The criminal laws of North Carolina are usually enforced on college campuses by campus police. These officials are not "security guards" like you might see at a mall. They are fully trained and licensed police officers who have full powers of arrest for violations of the law. They are authorized to execute these powers on campus and college-owned property (which may be "off-campus").

Local police officers ordinarily do not come on campus. However, they may be called to campus by the campus police officers if they need backup or if there is a crime that warrants it. In addition, in most college towns, the local police notify the campus police when students of the college violate the criminal law off-campus. Furthermore, it is important to note that fraternities, sororities, and many other student-affiliated sites may be located off-campus and are therefore under the supervision of local police.

In addition, there are law enforcement officers who work for the North Carolina Division of Alcohol Law Enforcement (known as "ALE"), a division of the Department of Crime Control and Public Safety. These officers are responsible for enforcing state laws regarding alcohol. The ALE officers come into contact with college students most frequently regarding the issue of underage drinking. These officers operate undercover and are often present in popular student bars and at sporting events and concerts. As employees of the State of North Carolina, they operate independently of the college. They are free to enter college property via public roads (and since roads often weave through campus, they have lots of access). The details of the alcohol laws that they enforce are discussed later in the book.

Your College Records

As a college student and adult, you will have certain rights under federal statutes and North Carolina state law that are designed to protect your privacy, both regarding your status as a student and any medical treatment that you might receive at school.

Medical Care

Unlike when you were under the age of 18, you now have authority to seek medical care or receive psychological counseling without involving your parents. Federal laws and the professional standards of the medical profession protect your confidentiality.

> **? Did You Know** that you do not have to receive parental consent to seek medical treatment or receive psychological counseling after you are 18?

Students often seek medical or psychological assistance from college professionals for intimate matters that they may wish to keep confidential. College students may have issues arise that involve sexual matters, drug or alcohol abuse, anxiety or depression, eating disorders, or troubled relationships with parents – to name just a few. Students should not hesitate to take advantage of the medical and psychological resources on campus if they are in need. In all but the rarest circumstances (such as risk of harm to yourself or others), any treatment you receive will remain confidential.

In most cases, your medical records – whether housed at your school's student health clinic or at an outside clinic – are confidential. The federal Health Insurance Portability and Accountability Act (HIPAA) sets out clear guidelines regarding medical privacy. Medical records are also regulated under the North Carolina laws that govern the licensure of medical professionals. It is presumed that medical records are confidential. Each school and student health clinic is required to have explicit documentation of its privacy policies; if you have specific questions about who can access your records and under what circumstances others can gain access, ask your school or clinic for a copy of its policy. If you don't understand how the policy actually works, ask someone on staff to explain it to you.

❗ Pay Attention!

If you use your parents' health insurance to pay for medical services, your parents will receive an "Explanation of Benefits" from the insurance company. While this report is rarely detailed, it will show that you received medical treatment, lab tests, etc. This information is related to the insurance coverage and technically is not a medical record.

At most schools, while campus medical care is not covered by tuition and fees and will be an additional charge to the student, psychological counseling is normally provided without additional charge. Ask how the billing works. If you have any concerns that information regarding your seeking psychological treatment might be sent to your parents due to billing practices, you can ask for an alternative way to pay.

Academic Records

Your student academic records are governed by the Family Educational Rights and Privacy Act (FERPA). When you were in high school, your parents (as your guardians) exercised your rights as a student under FERPA. When you turn 18 years old or enter a postsecondary institution at any age, all rights afforded to your parents under FERPA transfer to you, the "eligible student." However, be aware that FERPA provides ways in which a school may – but is not required to – share information from your education records with parents, without your consent.

- Schools may disclose education records to your parents if a health or safety emergency involves you.

- A school official may generally share with your parent information that is based on that official's personal knowledge or observation of you.

- Schools may inform your parents if you are under 21 years old and violate any law or policy concerning the use or possession of alcohol or a controlled substance.

- Schools may disclose education records to your parents if you are claimed as a dependent for tax purposes.

Contractual Obligations

The contracts that you sign with your college or university will govern the details of your student relationship. You sign a contract when you sign your application and when you sign a Housing Agreement. The details of these contracts are set out in the Student Handbook, which likely includes both a Code of Student Conduct and an Honor Code. There may be an additional publication setting out the details regarding your Housing Agreement, or it may be regulated under the Code of Student Conduct.

Student Conduct

Rules of student conduct will vary widely from large public universities to small, religiously affiliated private colleges. It is completely irrelevant that your friend did something at her college and only got 10 hours of community service from her school's Dean's Office while you did the same thing and were expelled from your school. *Each college is governed by its own contractual terms.*

Did You Know that colleges have virtually complete discretion to establish whatever rules of conduct they wish to apply at their schools?

The procedures that the college will follow in a disciplinary hearing are set out in the Student Handbook. *Public universities* must make sure that their procedures conform to the United States Constitution. (They inevitably do.) However, *private universities* are not governed by the United States Constitution. The **state action doctrine** holds that the Constitution only applies to arms of the government. Thus, the conduct of disciplinary hearings in private colleges is governed completely by contract – the procedures set out in the Student Handbook. More information and explanation about your Constitutional rights can be found later in this book.

Student Housing

Did You Know that if you are evicted from student housing for violating the rules, you typically will not get any of your money back for that semester?

The same ideas surrounding student conduct apply to housing regulations. For example, some schools allow students to let friends spend the night in campus housing. Other schools will evict you if you have an overnight guest. Each school sets its own standards.

You were given a copy of the Student Handbook
and a copy of the housing regulations, either in hard
copy or through an electronic link. Many (okay,
most) people do not read them. Do not be one of
those people! Read them as carefully as you read
the instructions to the SATs. Then read them again.
All persons living on campus will have Residence
Hall Directors and Resident Advisors (RAs),
usually older students employed by the residence
life office at your school. In other words, they may
be students, but they are also college employees
bound by the rules and regulations of their job.
Discuss all rules in the Student Handbook with
your RA if you have any questions. Remember,
ignorance is no defense!

❗ Pay Attention!

Your Student Handbook is a *must-read.*
Your school is notifying you of your responsibilities
and obligations as a student and what the school
can do if you don't follow them.

Moral Obligations

Finally, you are regulated by the moral standards
of your campus community. As mentioned above,
criminal laws are specific. Contractual rights and
responsibilities are specifically set out in Student
Handbooks and Housing Agreements. However,
many colleges also have Honor Codes, which
are intentionally quite vague. The full range of
offenses in Honor Codes is often not set out. They
typically prohibit lying, cheating, and stealing in

an academic context. Plagiarism is a serious matter that can have a devastating impact on your college record. Many times Honor Codes are enforced by students who sit on an Honor Council. You must talk to older students and quickly learn the values and habits of the students at your college, as there are a wide variety of approaches to the enforcement of Honor Codes. You need to learn how the one at your school operates. Once again, *ignorance is no defense!*

II. The System

Chapter 2
An Overview of Crime, Court, and Punishment

Overview of Crimes

Most people have a general idea that it is against the law to commit certain bad acts, such as murder. However, many people do not know how or why certain acts are classified as crimes. A **crime** is an act of doing something that violates a written law and may be punished by the state. For example, possessing marijuana is an act of doing something that violates a written law. A crime may also involve the failure to do something required by written law. For example, a parent who fails to give a baby nourishment violates a written law. All crimes are defined by written laws, called **statutes**. Statutes are made by a governing body, such as the legislature of a state.

Most of the crimes discussed in this book are violations of North Carolina state law and were enacted by the North Carolina legislature. Definitions of crimes in North Carolina can be found in the **General Statutes of North Carolina**. The United States Congress also makes laws, some of which are criminal statutes. However, most of the laws that affect college students in this state are North Carolina laws. This book will primarily discuss laws passed by the North Carolina legislature.

This book refers to a person who commits a crime as a **defendant**, a **perpetrator**, or an **offender**. This book refers to a person against whom a crime is committed as a **victim**.

Not knowing something was a crime does not get you off the hook. *Ignorance of the law is no defense.* The fact that police officers, prosecutors, defense attorneys, and judges in this state cannot recite from memory all of the criminal laws in North Carolina is not an excuse. (While researching this book, we found several laws we never knew existed, and we have each been lawyers for over 25 years!)

? Did You Know that giving a prescription drug to a friend may be a felony?

Example: *P1 has a valid prescription for Tylenol III® with Codeine. While in the dining hall during lunch, P1 gives one Tylenol III® pill to P2, who is not feeling well. P1 is guilty of distributing a Schedule V drug, which is a felony, with punishment of a minimum of 4 to 6 months of community punishment (probation, fines, community service, or substance treatment) or prison time. P2 is also guilty of a misdemeanor for possessing a Schedule V drug without a valid prescription.*

Prior to P1's arrest, P1 did not know that Tylenol III® is a Schedule V drug or that giving a Schedule V drug to another person is a felony. P1 cannot use ignorance of the law as a defense.

Example: *P is 18 years old. P hooks up with V, whom P thinks is 16 years old. V tells P that V is 16, and V looks at least that age. P has sexual intercourse with V. Turns out, V is actually 13 years old. P is guilty of statutory rape. Prior to P's arrest, P did not know that P could be charged with statutory rape if P made an honest mistake about a partner's age. P cannot use either ignorance of the statutory rape law or an honest mistake of fact (that V was 16 years old or older) as a defense.*

? Did You Know
that you may be charged with statutory rape even if the other person tells you that he or she is 16 years old or older?

This book describes crimes college students need to know, including some of the more serious crimes and consequences of violating them. However, do not rely on this book for all your knowledge of North Carolina's criminal laws. If you have a question regarding whether an act is a crime, you should consult an experienced criminal lawyer.

If you do not think something described in this book should be a crime, or if you think the punishment does not fit the crime, then write to your elected representatives or campaign to elect someone to change the law. Or, better yet, get elected to the legislature and get the law changed yourself! Do not violate the law just because you do not think something should be a crime.

Types of Courts

The trial courts in North Carolina are organized as superior courts and district courts. There are

46 superior court divisions and 42 district court divisions. The **superior court** handles felonies. The **district court** handles misdemeanors and juvenile cases. A person charged with a crime as an adult in superior court or district court has the right to a jury trial if the person faces a sentence of six months or more in prison.

Types of Crimes and Punishment

A **felony** is the name given to serious crimes for which the punishment is imprisonment in the State's prison system, life imprisonment, or death. Any crime can be declared a felony by statute. In North Carolina, felonies are prosecuted in superior courts by **district attorney** offices. A person convicted of a felony is a **felon**.

A **misdemeanor** is the name given to any crime that is not a felony (usually less serious crimes). In North Carolina, misdemeanors are prosecuted in district court by district attorney offices. A person convicted of a misdemeanor is a **misdemeanant**.

Punishment for a felony or misdemeanor may be **imprisonment**, **probation**, and/or a **fine**. You can learn more about different types of punishment in Chapter Five of this book.

The **state legislature** determines whether a crime in North Carolina is a felony or misdemeanor as well as the punishment for the crime, including whether a crime has a mandatory sentence or a specific fine.

A city or county **ordinance** is a law passed by the governing authority of a city or county. Violations may result in imprisonment, probation, and/or a fine. The maximum amount of jail time for violation of a city or county ordinance is six months.

Important Notes About Punishments Listed in this Book

Imprisonment only: The punishments address possible imprisonment, not possible fines.

First time offenses: The punishments apply the first time a person commits a crime. Repeated offenses of a crime will usually result in more severe punishments.

Probation option: Based on the structured sentencing guidelines outlined in Chapter Five, the judge may have the option of sentencing a party to probation rather than active jail time.

Failure to comply: Some jail sentences listed as punishments only apply if a person does not follow the terms of intermediate punishment (supervised probation) or community punishment. *See Chapter Five, Going to Trial and Getting Sentenced.*

Statutes of limitations: A statute of limitations

is a time limit or deadline imposed by the law regulating when a civil lawsuit must be filed or a criminal prosecution must be started.

- **Criminal Law**: In general, misdemeanors must be prosecuted within 2 years of the criminal act. If the prosecution is not started within that 2-year period, the perpetrator can never be prosecuted – even if the perpetrator is completely guilty. However, there is no statute of limitations regarding the prosecution of a felony. A silly mistake made in college can be a source of worry for years, and an actual prosecution could rear its ugly head years later. The passage of time presents no legal barrier to the State's ability to prosecute crimes that are felonies. As noted throughout the book, many actions that you might not consider to be that serious are in fact categorized as felonies under North Carolina law.

- **Civil Law**: In contrast, if you feel you have been injured in a civil matter, you need to contact an attorney regarding taking legal action or your claim may be barred. Civil statutes of limitations for many common problems are 3 years, but some issues have only a 1-year statute of limitations. Some claims based on statutory rights require you to give the opposing party notice within 180 days.

Chapter 3
Prosecution as an Adult

Sweet Sixteen

When you woke up on your 16th birthday, you may have celebrated – perhaps even on reality television – that you were Sweet 16 and eligible to drive. But, in North Carolina, your 16th birthday is also significant for another reason: from that point forward, you *must* be prosecuted and punished as an *adult* if you commit a crime in North Carolina. (If you commit a crime in North Carolina, the North Carolina rule applies regardless of the rule in your home state.) North Carolina is the only state in the United States that requires 16 year olds to be treated as adults under criminal laws. (In most other states, the age is 18.) On your 16th birthday, even though you were still restricted from voting, drinking alcohol, and buying cigarettes, you became an adult under North Carolina's criminal laws.

In determining whether or not you are tried as an adult, the age at which you commit the offense is the relevant age. If you commit an offense at age 15 but are not arrested until age 16, you will still be tried as a juvenile.

Any arrest that you receive after reaching your 16th birthday may remain on your criminal history

> **? Did You Know**
> that when you turn 16 years old, you are treated as an adult under North Carolina's criminal laws and can go to an adult prison and have a criminal record for the rest of your life?

record for the remainder of your life. You will probably have to provide a copy of your criminal history record when you apply for a job, apply for courses or study abroad programs at other schools, or apply to graduate school. If you are able to have your case dismissed, you may be able to get the arrest expunged from your criminal history record.

> **Example:** *P, who is 17 years old, is a first-year college student from Alabama. **P** is arrested for shoplifting in North Carolina and is prosecuted as an adult. If **P** had committed the crime in Alabama, **P** would have been prosecuted as a juvenile.*

Expunction/Erasing Your Record

If you are less than 18 years old and plead guilty to or are found guilty of a *misdemeanor* and it is your first conviction of any crime (excluding traffic violations), you may apply to have the conviction **expunged** (*i.e.*, erased) from your record.

Additionally, if you are less than 21 years old and plead guilty to or are found guilty of misdemeanor possession of alcohol and it is your first conviction of any crime (excluding traffic violations), you may apply to have the conviction expunged from your record.

There is no guarantee that the record will be expunged, and you only get one chance to apply for **expunction**.

❗ Pay Attention!

Expunction is available *only* for misdemeanors, not felonies. As noted throughout the book, many actions that you might not consider to be that serious are in fact categorized as felonies under North Carolina law.

Chapter 4
Parties to a Crime (Who Can Be Charged?)

 Did You Know that you can be guilty of a criminal act if you encourage another person to commit the act, and the other person commits the act, even if you were not present when the crime was committed?

There are many ways that you might get punished for a crime even if *you* don't actually commit it. This can occur if you help plan or help commit a crime, whether it is a felony or a misdemeanor.

Accessory Before the Fact

Crime: A crime occurs when a person counsels, procures, or commands the principal actor to commit a felony even though the person is *not* present when the principal actually commits the felony. The person is guilty as an accessory before the fact.

Punishment: Same as the principal actor

Example: P1 (a tech genius) shows P2 how to make fake driver's licenses. P2 proceeds to make and sell fake driver's licenses to persons under 21 years old who intend to use them to purchase alcohol. P2 is guilty of a Class I Felony for selling a simulation of a driver's license. P1 is guilty as an accessory before the fact and is subject to the same punishment as P2.

Conspiracy

Crime: The crime of conspiracy occurs when two or more persons agree to commit an unlawful act, or agree to do a lawful act in an unlawful way or by unlawful means.

The crime is the *agreement*. No steps need be taken to commit the crime.

A person may be convicted of and punished for both conspiracy and the substantive offense which the person conspired to commit, if the offense is in fact committed.

Punishment: One class lower than the crime that the person conspired to commit

> **Example:** *P1, P2, and P3 decide to purchase an ounce of marijuana to share between them. P1 calls a local dealer and arranges to meet the dealer to pick up the marijuana. When P1 goes to meet the dealer, the police, who have been following the dealer, arrest P1 before the purchase is complete. P1, P2, and P3 are all guilty of conspiracy to purchase marijuana.*

Did You Know that you can be guilty of conspiracy if you plan to commit a crime with your friends even if the crime is never actually committed?

Accessory After the Fact

Crime: A crime occurs if, after a felony has been committed, a person with knowledge of the felony aids the felon in any manner to escape arrest or punishment. The person is guilty as an accessory after the fact.

Did You Know that you can be guilty of a crime for helping your friend avoid arrest?

Punishment: Same as the principal felon

Aiding and Abetting

P1 sees P2's girlfriend, V, making out with another guy on the couch at a party. P1 calls P2, who isn't there, and tells him. P2 asks P1 to keep a look out while P2 comes to the party and keys V's car. P1 stops V from leaving when he sees her about to walk out the front door. P2 is guilty of willful and wanton injury to personal property, and P1 is guilty for aiding and abetting. Both will receive the same punishment for willful and wanton injury to personal property.

 Crime: The crime of aiding and abetting occurs when a person knowingly advises, encourages, or aids the principal actor to commit a crime, and the person's actions contribute to the commission of the crime by the principal actor.

While accessory before the fact and accessory after the fact only apply to felonies, aiding and abetting applies to *all* offenses.

 Punishment: Same as the principal actor

> **Example:** *P1, the president of his fraternity, tells an 18-year-old first-year pledge, P2, to purchase beer for the annual frat house beach party. P2, while purchasing beer with a fake ID, is arrested. P2 is guilty of underage possession of alcohol and use of a fake ID. The*

> *frat president, **P1**, is also guilty of aiding and abetting. **P1** is subject to the same punishment as **P2**.*

If two people join together to commit a crime, each of them is guilty as a principal if the other commits that particular crime. In addition, each person is also guilty of any other crime committed when either of them carries out the crime, or any other crime that occurs as a natural or probable consequence of the crime.

> **Example:** *P1 and P2 go to a house party together and plan to steal iPods and laptops from the house. **P1** plans to wait outside with the car running, and **P2** plans to go in, get the items while everyone is busy partying, and come out. While inside, **P2** gets caught by one of the roommates and engages in a fistfight that causes the roommate to end up in a coma. **P1** and **P2** will both be punished for felony larceny and felonious assault, Class H and Class F felonies. It does not matter that **P1** had nothing to do with the fight and did not know **P2** would engage in a fight that resulted in serious bodily injury to the roommate.*

In some cases, college students argue that they should not be charged with a crime because they did not actually "participate" in the crime – rather, their roommates or sorority sisters or teammates or the designated driver did. However, all persons involved in committing, planning, participating, helping, advising, encouraging, or benefiting in the criminal activity are parties to the crime. If you had anything to do with committing the crime, no matter how minor the involvement might have been, you may be convicted of the crime.

In addition, you can be guilty of aiding and abetting when you make it possible for others to break the law.

Example: *P is studying in P's dorm room one night when some of P's friends, all under the age of 21, show up with a case of beer. They offer P a beer, which P declines, though P allows them to stay in P's room and break open the case. P is guilty of aiding and abetting underage consumption of alcohol by knowingly providing P's friends a location in which to break the law.*

Pay Attention!
When your friends do a crime, you may also be punished.

Chapter 5
Going to Trial and Getting Sentenced

Suggestions if You Are Summoned to Court

The following are some suggestions if you receive a **summons** to appear in court because you received a traffic violation or a county ordinance violation or because you are arrested for a crime:

• Consult with an attorney about your situation. A brief consultation with an attorney may be free of charge; however, clarify payment issues before beginning the conversation. You may or may not actually have to hire an attorney, depending on how serious and/or complicated your case is.

• Always appear in court on your court date if you are required to go to court. Even if you do not have an attorney, you must answer the summons to appear in court by showing up. If you fail to appear in court on your court date, an order for your arrest will be issued, you will be arrested, and your eventual punishment may be increased. Don't complicate your situation by forgetting to show up. If you fail to show up for a traffic infraction, the Department of Motor Vehicles (DMV) will suspend your license, and you will probably incur additional fines and fees.

• Arrive early when you go to court – you may get to go first, which could save you a lot of time. Not to mention, if you're late and they have already called your case, you may be considered a no-show, and the judge may issue an order for your arrest.

- Dress appropriately. Our suggestion is to dress as if you are going to a religious service or a funeral. When you dress nicely, you are showing respect to the judge [*i.e.*, be sure your pants are pulled up, your shirt is tucked in (wear collared shirts, not t-shirts), and your clothing is modest].

- Do not take cell phones or pagers into a courtroom.

- Do not wear a cap or a hat in the courtroom.

- Do not chew gum or take any food or drink into a courtroom.

- Always be respectful and look the judge in the eye. Answer with "Yes, Your Honor" or "No, Your Honor" when being questioned by the judge.

Proof of Guilt and Jury Trials

The **prosecutor** must be able to prove that a person accused of a crime is **guilty beyond a reasonable doubt**. A person may also admit guilt and plead guilty to a crime.

You have the right under the Sixth Amendment to the United States Constitution to have your guilt decided by a jury if you face a sentence of six months or more in prison. A person may waive the right to a jury trial and have guilt or innocence determined by a judge.

Overview of Structured Sentencing in North Carolina

North Carolina has a system of structured sentencing for all misdemeanors and felonies. Depending on which level of crime you commit, the judge will refer to the misdemeanor and felony sentencing charts to determine the minimum and maximum **sentence**. The judge has the discretion to choose a sentence within that range.

Based on the crime, a judge may sentence you to active, intermediate, or community punishment. For some crimes, jail time is mandatory.

Active punishment for persons who commit felonies requires incarceration in the state prison system. Active punishment for persons who commit misdemeanors will result in incarceration in the state prison system for sentences of 90 days or more and in the county jail for sentences of fewer than 90 days.

Intermediate punishment is supervised probation with one or more of the following: split sentencing (jail time plus community options), electronic house arrest, intensive supervision, a residential center, a day reporting center, or a drug treatment center.

Community punishment does not involve prison, jail, or an intermediate punishment. Instead, it may include one or more of the following: fines,

restitution (*i.e.*, monetary reimbursement), community service, or substance abuse treatment.

Sentencing Guidelines

North Carolina judges must comply with **sentencing guidelines** (outlined in the following charts) when sentencing convicted offenders.

The charts simplify the sentencing guidelines used by judges, and they only show the usual range for first-time offenders of both felonies and misdemeanors. Both felonies and misdemeanors are broken down into level of offense. Felonies range from level A to level I. Misdemeanors range from level A1 to level 3.

Each level of offense has a corresponding punishment. Not to be confused by the letters designating the level of offense, the type of punishment possible for each level is indicated by A for active, I for intermediate, or C for community. If all three are listed, the judge has the option of picking any of the three.

The possible minimum sentences are also listed in the following charts. Once a judge determines the minimum sentence, the maximum sentence is at least 20% longer.

Throughout this book, the description of each offense includes the level of the offense.

Felony Punishment Chart

Level of Offense	Length of Minimum Sentence	Type of Punishment
A	Death or Life Without Parole	A
B1	192-240 months	A
B2	125-157 months	A
C	58-73 months	A
D	51-64 months	A
E	20-25 months	I / A
F	13-16 months	I / A
G	10-13 months	I / A
H	5-6 months	C / I / A
I	4-6 months	C

Misdemeanor Punishment Chart

Level of Offense	Length of Minimum Sentence	Type of Punishment
A1	1-60 Days	C / I / A
1	1-45 Days	C
2	1-80 Days	C
3	1-10 Days	C

Minimum Term Length

In North Carolina, persons who are convicted of crimes and sentenced to incarceration must serve 100% of their minimum term. Minimum sentences cannot be reduced for "good behavior." Prisoners do not earn good time, gain time, or **parole** before completing the minimum sentence.

Community Punishment

If you are assigned a community punishment, the active term is suspended. However, if you are sentenced to community punishment, make sure you follow your sentencing to the letter. If you fail to comply with the community punishment, you can be sent to jail or prison for the minimum term assigned by the judge.

Imprisonment

If you are sentenced to spend time in prison, factors such as your age, the type of crime, and the judge's sentence determine where you will serve the sentence.

Between the ages of 13 and 18, if you are tried and sentenced as an adult, you will most likely start serving your sentence in a prison facility for young offenders in Morganton. If you are at least 18 years old and are sentenced to fewer than 90 days in jail, you will serve the time in the county jail. If you are at least 18 years old and are sentenced to more than 90 days in jail, you will serve the time in a state prison.

Probation

Probation is punishment served outside of prison, but there's a catch. Probation is usually conditioned on certain restrictions or requirements, including one or more of the following:

- Payment of a probation supervision fee to a probation officer;

- Payment of a fine;

- Payment of restitution, if any, to the victim;

- No use of alcohol or drugs;

- Random drug and alcohol tests;

- Community service;

- Avoidance of people of bad character (such as other people who may be on probation); OR

- Waiver of rights protected by the Fourth

Amendment to the United States Constitution.

The last condition above means that a probation officer or law enforcement officer can search you, your home, and your car without a search warrant or probable cause while you are on probation.

If a judge decides that you have violated a condition of probation, the judge can sentence you to spend the rest or a portion of the remaining sentence in prison.

> **Example:** *P is convicted of selling Vicodin®
> to classmates, a Class H Felony. The judge
> sentences **P** to supervised probation and
> requires **P** to participate in a drug treatment
> program. **P** fails to attend the drug treatment
> program and is sent to prison to serve, at the
> very least, a minimum sentence of 5 months in
> prison.*

Fines

Judges may impose fines for felonies and misdemeanors in addition to other punishment. Fines for most misdemeanors typically do not exceed $1,000. Fines for most felonies exceed $1,000 and may be $100,000 or greater, depending on the crime.

III. Search, Arrest, and Speech: Your Rights Under the Constitution

Chapter 6
Your Constitutional Rights: Search and Seizure

Several students were hanging out in front of the campus student union. A town police officer approached the students and asked for their names. The officer then asked one of the students if the officer could see the contents of the student's pockets, and the student emptied his pockets. The student had a pill in his pocket that turned out to be Ritalin®. A friend had given him the pill earlier that day. The student was immediately arrested for possession of a Schedule II drug without a prescription.

When the student's attorney later asked him, "Why did you empty your pockets?", the student replied that he thought he was always supposed to do what a police officer asked. In this case, the officer did not have probable cause to search the student's pockets, but the evidence from the search was admissible in court because the student allowed the officer to see the contents of his pockets.

The Fourth Amendment to the **United States Constitution** protects you against "unreasonable searches and seizures." Additionally, the Fifth Amendment to the United States Constitution protects you against **self-incrimination**. The Sixth

? Did You Know that if a police officer asks permission to search you, your pockets, your car, your book bag, or anything else that belongs to you, you always have the right to refuse to consent to the search?

Amendment to the United States Constitution grants the right to a jury trial and the right to an attorney.

The **United States Supreme Court**, the highest court in this country, has interpreted these Amendments in many cases. Interpretations of law by the Supreme Court are applicable to everyone in the United States. The discussions in Chapters Six and Seven are based in part on interpretations of the Fourth, Fifth, and Sixth Amendments by the United States Supreme Court.

Law students usually spend at least one entire semester of law school trying to learn the law on search and seizure of people and property and the laws involving an arrest. In the next couple of chapters, we explain some of the basic principles to give you an understanding of your rights. If you have any questions regarding your rights in a particular situation, you should consult with a lawyer.

Requirement of Probable Cause

All persons are protected by the Fourth Amendment to the United States Constitution against unreasonable searches and seizures by governmental authorities. In almost all cases, a police officer must have probable cause to search a person or property (including a vehicle). **Probable cause** exists when a reasonable person would believe that a crime was committed or that evidence of a crime is at a particular location. Probable cause requires more than suspicion. A police officer does not always have to get a search warrant before conducting a search. However, the police officer must have probable cause for the search, with certain limited exceptions. One of these exceptions is if you consent to the search.

Consent to Searches

A college student is standing on a street corner in the middle of the afternoon. A police officer asks if the officer can look inside the student's messenger bag. The student could respond, "No, I do not consent to a search of my messenger bag." The student could also say, "I would like to call my lawyer [or the Dean of Students or another trusted (older) adult]." If the police officer insists on continuing with a search, the student should be respectful and cooperative. Later, if the student is arrested, the student should get an attorney and tell the attorney that the student did not consent to the search.

If a police officer has probable cause, the officer is not required to ask your permission to search you, your vehicle, or your belongings.

However, many times a police officer will ask you for consent (or permission) to search you, your vehicle, or your belongings. The officer makes this request because if you give consent, the officer is not required to have probable cause to conduct the search – you just gave the officer permission to do so. If a police officer asks you for permission to search, you have the right to refuse to consent. Many people do not realize they have this right and tend to consent to whatever a police officer requests.

If a police officer asks you to consent to a search of you or your belongings, and you give consent, a judge will usually find the search to be valid even if the officer could not have established probable cause for the search. Your consent will generally be enough to make a search lawful, even if the search may otherwise have been unlawful. However, if you do not consent to a search, and the police officer cannot show probable cause to a judge, the judge can find that the search is not valid.

❗ Pay Attention!

If an officer asks for your consent to search you, your vehicle, or your belongings, you have the right to refuse to consent to the search. If you exercise this right, you should state clearly and respectfully that you do not consent. If the officer proceeds with a search, you should continue to be respectful, and you should not interfere with the search (or you may be guilty of obstruction of justice). Be sure to tell your attorney later that you did not consent to the search.

Other Rules on Consent

- A child does not have the right to consent to a search of a parent's home.

- A parent has the right to give police consent to search a child's room in the parent's home or a child's car if owned by the parent. Even if you think it is your room because you do not share it with anyone, if it is in your parent's or guardian's house, your parent or guardian can give permission for the police to search the room without your consent to the search.

- A driver has the right to give an officer consent to search a vehicle. This rule applies even if the car is registered in someone else's name.

Searches of People

Someone reports seeing a person on campus with what appears to be a handgun and gives a description of the person to the police. A police officer arrives and sees a person who resembles the description. The police officer can stop the person and pat down the person's outer clothing for the officer's own safety. If the officer feels something that resembles a handgun inside the person's clothing, the officer can conduct a full search.

If a police officer has a **reasonable suspicion** that criminal activity has just taken place or is about to take place, the police officer may stop you and ask you questions. Reasonable suspicion is based on more than a hunch, but less than probable cause. If and only if the police officer has reason to believe that you are armed and dangerous, the police officer can conduct a frisk. A **frisk** is a pat-down of your outer clothing. If and only if the officer develops probable cause during the frisk that evidence of a crime (such as drugs or weapons) is present, then the officer has the right to search you.

After a police officer arrests a person for a crime, the officer has the right to search the person. The police officer does not need probable cause to search a person who is under arrest.

> **Example:** *The police arrest P for shoplifting. The police search P's pockets and find marijuana. The police do not need probable cause to search P's pockets because P is under arrest.*

A school has the right to require drug testing of every student who participates in a school-sanctioned extracurricular activity, such as sports or clubs, as outlined in the school's guidelines for participation (*e.g.,* waivers for intramural sports). In these instances, drug testing is not considered a search under the law. Rather, drug testing is considered a condition of being allowed to participate in an activity. Think of it as similar to flying on an airplane. As a condition of allowing you to fly, the airport has the right to search you and your luggage.

❶ Pay Attention!
The NCAA and the college athletic conferences have rules governing participation in varsity college athletics. If you are a varsity athlete, you are bound by both the rules of your school and the rules of the organizations that govern college athletics.

❗ Pay Attention!

In the case of alcohol consumption, probable cause is relatively easy for police officers to get. For instance, tripping on the sidewalk or smelling like alcohol can be used as probable cause for an officer to request you to take a breathalyzer test.

> **Example:** *P, an 18-year-old first-year student, is walking home to P's dorm late at night on a Friday. A police officer is standing on the sidewalk near the entrance to the residence hall and asks P for P's name. After P responds, the officer tells P that the officer smells alcohol and asks for P to take a breathalyzer test. P agrees, and the breathalyzer registers alcohol in P's system. P is arrested for underage consumption of alcohol.*

❗ Pay Attention!

Just because an officer has probable cause to believe you have been drinking does not mean you have to consent to a breathalyzer test. You have a Constitutional right to refuse to consent to take a breathalyzer test. *However, you need to be aware that under current North Carolina law, your refusal to consent could be used as evidence against you in court.*

Searches of Vehicles

A state trooper stopped a student for speeding on the highway near campus. When the state trooper approached the vehicle, the trooper smelled

? Did You Know
that if the
police stop you for a
traffic violation, or at a
traffic stop checkpoint,
they can search you and
your vehicle if they see or
smell evidence of drugs or
alcohol?

marijuana in the car. The trooper ordered the driver and the passenger to exit the vehicle and then conducted a search of the vehicle for drugs. The trooper found marijuana in the glove box between the driver and the passenger and arrested both for possession of marijuana.

Police must have a reason before they can stop a vehicle. For example, if the officer sees a traffic offense (*e.g.*, a tail light is out, the tag is outdated, or the driver rolls through a stop sign), the officer has a reason to stop the vehicle. Police may also stop a vehicle if they have a reasonable suspicion that the vehicle was involved in criminal activity. In addition, police may establish a valid roadblock to check every driver who passes through the checkpoint.

After the officer stops a vehicle for a valid reason, the officer may order the driver out of the vehicle even if the officer does not have reason to believe that the driver is involved in criminal activity. The officer may also order passengers out of the vehicle and search them in appropriate circumstances. The passengers also have Fourth Amendment rights. Police may, in certain circumstances, search vehicles without a search warrant.

! Pay Attention!
Police may search a vehicle if, after making a valid stop, the officer has probable cause to believe that evidence of a crime (*e.g.*, drugs) is present.

Example: *P, who is under 21 years old, is driving an SUV with a burned-out tail light. An officer stops P's car and sees beer through the back window of the SUV's back hatch. Beer in the possession of a person under 21 years old is a crime, even if the person has not been drinking. The officer may search P's car without a warrant.*

❗ Pay Attention!

Police may search a vehicle if the officer arrests a driver or passenger and has probable cause to believe that evidence of the crime is in the car.

Example: *P is driving a car erratically. The police stop P's car, smell alcohol on P's breath, and arrest P for driving under the influence. The police may search P's car for drugs or alcohol without a warrant.*

❗ Pay Attention!

Police may search a vehicle if the officer impounds a vehicle after arresting the driver.

Example: *P is arrested for reckless driving and taken into custody. There are no passengers in the car. The police may impound P's car and search it later at the impound lot without a warrant.*

❗ Pay Attention!

When you register your car for parking on campus, you are bound by campus rules regarding the search of vehicles. At some colleges, on-campus vehicle registration may enable school police officers to search your vehicle without probable cause. Read your Student Handbook.

Searches in Student Housing

? Did You Know that if a college employee – such as an RA – is conducting a routine check of rooms and sees alcohol or drugs in plain view, you could be subject to both criminal and college punishment?

As mentioned above, the Fourth Amendment to the United States Constitution protects your privacy. As a general rule, agents of the government (*e.g.,* police officers) cannot enter your dwelling without having probable cause to believe that they will find evidence of a crime. The protection clearly applies when you live in a private home. The situation is more complicated when you live in student housing. While it has been mentioned that the Constitution does not apply at private colleges due to the absence of state or governmental action, private colleges routinely behave as if it did *with regard to searches.*

A Room of (Not) Your Own

Since the university or college owns the dorm, it can set out the conditions of your occupancy in your Housing Agreement. You do *not* have total control over your room. Members of the college staff (usually RAs, and sometimes campus police) have master keys to all rooms, and they are free to enter at any time to ensure the health, safety, or welfare of a student – for example, if someone smells fire. A typical situation may involve an RA who is properly in your room and sees evidence *in plain view* of a crime (a bong on your desk or a handle of vodka next to your sink if you are under

21) or a violation of the Housing Agreement (a hot plate or a pet). The RA calls the campus police about the criminal evidence, and the campus police arrive and seize the evidence in plain view. Under this scenario, you could be punished for university infractions as well as for criminal violations.

In addition, Housing Agreements commonly specify that RAs will inspect rooms for health and safety violations on a periodic basis (usually once a semester). Again, if an RA is properly in your room, anything improper in plain view subjects you to punishment.

When a Search of Your Room is Legal

A search by governmental agents (*e.g.,* police officers) is legal in only three circumstances:

- **Search warrant**: If the governmental agent has a warrant from a judge authorizing a complete search of your property because the agent had probable cause to believe you were committing or had committed a crime;

- **Plain view**: If the governmental agent had a legal reason to be in your room and, while there, sees evidence of a crime in plain view; OR

- **Consent**: If you give your consent to a search when asked. You do *not* have to give consent to search to a governmental agent. Remember, a police officer may request your consent in situations where the officer does not otherwise have probable cause.

Search Warrants

Campus police at *public universities*, as governmental agents, must obtain a search warrant to search your room for evidence of criminal wrongdoing. Campus police at *private universities* are often deputized police offers, and they often procure search warrants. In both public and private universities, you have the right to refuse to give your consent to a search of your room to a police officer who does not have a search warrant.

Plain View Doctrine

Most students get in trouble when they leave evidence of breaking the law in plain view in areas where college officials are present on legitimate business. Evidence could include beer cans in the recycling bin or a small amount of marijuana in an ashtray. Police officers are entitled to seize this evidence in plain view and use it against you in court. However, seeing evidence in plain view does not give a police officer the right to conduct a search of closed spaces unless the officer obtains a search warrant or you give the officer your consent.

Consents to Searches

Police can conduct a search without a search warrant and without probable cause if you consent to the search. Giving consent to a search has the potential of turning a minor infraction into a major crisis. If a police officer sees contraband in your room in plain view, the officer does not have the authority to open closed spaces in your room (*e.g.,* a drawer, closet, or book bag) unless the officer obtains a search warrant or you give the officer your consent.

The officer would have to obtain a search warrant from a judge. If you give your consent, the officer may conduct a full search of your room, and any evidence found of any possible criminal activity may be used against you. If you do not give your consent, and the officer proceeds to search your room anyway without a search warrant, anything found in that search may not be admissible against you in a criminal trial.

The Fine Print in Housing Agreements

Your housing agreement may state that you must consent to a search if requested by a school authority. If you refuse to consent to the search and contraband is discovered, the contraband may be used as evidence by school officials in school disciplinary proceedings. You may be evicted from student housing, or even suspended or expelled from school. However, if you refuse consent, and the search of your room is conducted without a search warrant by a deputized police officer (including campus police), any evidence seized will likely *not* be admissible in a state criminal trial. If you consent to a search of your room, any evidence found is admissible in both state criminal courts and in school proceedings.

But That Belongs to My Roommate...

Often in student housing, you will be living with other people. If they are violating legal or contractual duties, you could be held responsible as well if the authorities cannot determine who is in violation of the rules. Be sure to keep a clear division of your space if possible.

You have the right to consent to a police officer's search of a room you share with another person. On the flip side, your roommate has the right to consent to a search of your room, even if you are not present. However, if there is a clear division of personal items, the police officer may only search what belongs to the person who consented to the search and items found in a common area (*e.g.*, in your shared refrigerator or on your shared futon). If contraband is found in a common area, even if your roommate was the person who consented to the search (and even if the contraband does not belong to you), the evidence may possibly be used against both you *and* your roommate in criminal courts and school proceedings. As stated earlier, you also have the right to refuse to consent to a search if the police officer does not have a search warrant.

Example: *An RA is making a safety inspection of the suite you share with three others. There is a common living room and kitchen, a bath, and two bedrooms off the living room. You are in the living room alone when the RA arrives. The RA sees a joint and a scale and calls the campus police. Neither is yours. A campus police officer comes over, sees the joint and scale in plain view, and asks you if they are yours. You truthfully say no and that you do not know whose they are. He then asks you if he can open the drawers in a chest of drawers in the living room and open the door to a coat closet. He also asks you which bedroom is yours and asks to go through the drawers in your room. You share one of the bedrooms with another*

> *person. You know you and your roommate don't have any drugs in your bedroom. You could consent to a search of your bedroom if you wished. However, you cannot consent to a search of the other bedroom. You could also consent to a search of the common areas – the living room, kitchen, bath, and coat closet. However, you know that one of your other roommates has some pretty sketchy friends. You don't know whose scale it is or what might be in the drawers or the closet.*

In this example, you have the right to refuse to consent to a search. If the police were to find something serious (like enough marijuana to charge someone with possession with intent to sell rather than the simple misdemeanor possession of the visible joint), you are then in a position where you might be charged with a crime, too.

The Bottom Line

In short, if you possess illegal items in your dorm room, you could be subject to punishment from both your college (*e.g.,* suspension) *and* the State of North Carolina (*e.g.,* conviction in criminal court). If you are charged by the State with possession of an illegal item in your room, evidence of the item can only be used against you if it was properly seized by law enforcement. In other words, the police officers must have had probable cause and obtained a search warrant, seen the item in plain view, or obtained your consent to search. If the search was not legal, the item – no matter what it was or how incriminating – cannot be entered into evidence in court (and you cannot be convicted of possession of that item).

Chapter 7
Your Constitutional Rights: Arrest

Definition of Arrest and Police Questioning

A store manager sees a local college student in a store for a long period of time. The student is carrying several bags, even though she has not made any purchase. The store manager suspects that the student has shoplifted some items and calls the police. The police officer arrives and sees the student coming out of the store holding armfuls of shopping bags. The officer has reasonable suspicion that the student may be involved in criminal activity. The officer may stop her and inquire about her name. However, if the officer asks questions about other things, such as the contents of the bags, the student does not have to answer.

If the officer keeps the student for more than a brief period of time and requires her to stay in an office at the store for further questioning, and the student does not feel free to leave, the student is technically under "arrest," even if the officer does not say that the student is under arrest. The officer cannot continue questioning the student without reading the Miranda warnings to her. (Continue reading this chapter for a discussion of Miranda warnings.) The student is not required to answer any questions (beyond providing her name) and may ask to call her parents or another trusted (older) adult

? Did You Know that you do not have to be in handcuffs and the police officer does not have to say, "You are under arrest!" for you actually to be under arrest?

? Did You Know that if you are stopped by police for questioning, you do not have to provide any information other than your name?

(such as a dean, professor, college administrator, the person she babysits for after class, etc.). The student should request an attorney to be present before she answers any further questions.

Fortunately, most people who read this book will never be arrested. However, if you are arrested, you should know your rights under our laws. An **arrest** is the taking of a person into **custody** against the person's will for the purpose of criminal prosecution or interrogation. A police officer can only arrest you if the officer has probable cause to believe that you have committed a crime.

An arrest does not occur if a police officer simply approaches you and asks you questions. If a police officer has a reasonable suspicion that you may be involved in criminal activity, the officer may stop you and ask for your name. **Reasonable suspicion** is based on more than a hunch, but less than probable cause. After you provide your name to the officer, you are not obligated to answer any more questions. If you decide to answer questions beyond your name, the answers must be truthful. Giving false statements to law enforcement officials is a crime. However, it is important to know that law enforcement officials are not required to be truthful with you at all times.

❗ Pay Attention!

If you are the driver of a car, you have to provide a driver's license when pulled over by the police. If you are a passenger in a car or a pedestrian, a police officer can ask you to identify yourself (and you must truthfully provide your name), though you do not have to provide an identifying document (*e.g.*, a driver's license or college ID card) to the officer – even if the officer asks for it. You are also not required to provide your age or birth date to the officer. However, if you answer an officer's questions and are not honest about your identity or age, you are committing a crime.

If the officer continues questioning, and you are not free to leave, the stop may be considered an arrest. A police officer does not have to say, "You are under arrest!" to place you under arrest. The determining factor is, after a brief questioning, were you free to leave? If a reasonable person would have felt free to leave, the officer has not made an arrest.

❗ Pay Attention!

If in doubt, ask the police officer if you are free to leave. If the police officer says yes, do so.

An officer does not need an arrest warrant if the officer has probable cause to arrest you, or if you commit a crime in the officer's presence.

If you are arrested, the police officer must tell you about your *Miranda* warnings before asking you more questions.

Miranda Warnings

Every person who has ever seen a cop show on television has heard the term ***Miranda* warning**.

Miranda warnings are required because of a famous decision by the United States Supreme Court, *Miranda v. Arizona*. These warnings are cautionary instructions that law enforcement officials must give a person in custody before interrogation. You are in custody if a) a police officer places you under arrest, or b) a police officer questions you in a situation in which a reasonable person would not feel free to leave. You do not have to be at the police station to be in custody! You are in custody *anywhere* after you are under arrest. If you are in custody, the police must advise you of the following *Miranda* warnings:

- You have the right to remain silent;

- Anything you say can be used against you in a court of law;

- You have the right to have an attorney present during questioning;

- If you cannot afford an attorney, one will be appointed for you prior to questioning; AND

- You can terminate the questioning at any time and exercise any of these rights.

If you choose to exercise your right to remain silent, or you choose to speak only with a lawyer present, you must *state out loud* to the officer that you are exercising your right to remain silent, your right to an attorney, or both.

The police are not required to find you an attorney before they question you. However, if you are under arrest and you ask for an attorney, the police cannot ask you any more questions until your attorney is present. If you are arrested, the fact that you ask to have an attorney present before answering any questions cannot be used against you later by a judge or a jury.

❶ Pay Attention!
Police officers who are questioning you are allowed to lie to you or trick you as part of their investigation. If you are not under arrest, you do not have to answer any questions other than your name. If you are under arrest, *always* request an attorney to be present before answering any questions.

Chapter 8
Your Constitutional Rights: Speech and Other Issues

As mentioned in the previous two chapters, even college students have rights protected by the United States Constitution, as interpreted by the United States Supreme Court.

First Amendment Rights

The First Amendment to the United States Constitution protects your right to free speech. As previously mentioned, the Constitution does not apply at private colleges due to the absence of state action. Many private colleges act as if it does because they are committed to a free exchange of ideas. However, other schools can be committed to a particular viewpoint and operate the college to advance that viewpoint to the exclusion of others. For example, a private school could require a student to attend weekly chapel services or wear plaid kilts every Friday, while a public school could not. Private schools are free to do this because they are not arms of the government. And don't forget, you're choosing to go there, so if you have a huge thing against plaid kilts or religious services, you may choose to apply to enroll elsewhere.

Public Colleges and Student Organizations

At public colleges, all student organizations must be treated equitably. While *all* groups do not have to be treated *equally*, similar groups have to be treated in similar ways. The college cannot give extraordinary benefits to a student group based on the viewpoint that the group espouses. While colleges have discretion to give benefits to student groups at all, once they decide to do so, all groups must be treated equitably. For example, a college does not have to let students use classrooms for club meetings at all. However, if it does, it must allow all student organizations access to classrooms. If the college lists student groups on the official website, it cannot refuse to list some groups because the school disapproves of the messages of the groups. Guidelines for student organizations and university funding of organizations are often outlined in a student activities handbook. While a public school cannot legally discriminate against someone's views, it can have rules and restrictions for organizations so long as the school has a rational basis for its reasons (*e.g.*, a school may give more money to organizations with more people if the school's rules and restrictions for giving out funds provide that clubs with lots of members can get more money than clubs with fewer members). However, the process for applying for funds must treat each applicant equitably.

Funding Student Organizations

While a public college cannot legally engage in viewpoint discrimination, neither can you as a student. College tuition includes student fees, which the college uses to fund student activities. While a student might object that part of the fee is distributed to a campus group of which the student disapproves, the First Amendment does not provide a remedy. You may, though, form a campus group that advances your viewpoint and seek funding from your school.

IV. Substances: Alcohol, Drugs, and Driving

Chapter 9
Alcohol and Underage Drinking

The legal age to purchase and consume alcohol in North Carolina is 21. (You can consume alcohol if you are under 21 under very limited circumstances discussed below.)

One of the most frequent ways that persons under 21 years old get in trouble with the law in North Carolina is due to possession and/or consumption of alcohol. But not only persons under 21 years old get in trouble; sometimes other people (including parents) get in trouble when they allow persons under 21 years old to consume alcohol. This chapter describes common alcohol-related crimes that affect persons under 21 years old other than driving after consuming alcohol or drugs or impaired driving (DWI), which is discussed in Chapter Fourteen.

Purchase, Possession, or Consumption of Alcohol by Person Under 21 Years Old

Crime: A crime occurs when a person under 21 years old purchases, attempts to purchase, possesses, or consumes alcoholic beverages.

Type of Crime: Class 1 Misdemeanor

Did You Know that alcohol on the breath is enough evidence to charge a person under 21 years old with consumption of alcohol?

❓ Did You Know that conviction of underage purchase, possession, or consumption of alcohol results in a 1-year revocation of your driver's license?

⚖ Punishment: Community punishment with up to 45 days in jail for failure to comply *and* 1-year revocation of driver's license

Exceptions: A person under 21 years old does not commit a crime if the person:

- Possesses or uses alcohol provided by licensed physicians, druggists, or dental surgeons for medicinal or pharmaceutical purposes;

- Possesses or uses unfortified wine or fortified wine provided by an organized church or ordained minister for sacramental purposes;

- Possesses or uses alcohol during a culinary class as required by established culinary curriculum under the direct supervision of an instructor at an accredited college or university; OR

- Serves alcohol as part of the person's lawful employment if the person is 18-20 years old.

> **Example:** *A student is under 21 years old and is a member of the Catholic faith. The student is served wine during mass at the local Catholic church. The student is NOT violating the law.*

Exceptions for 19- and 20-year-olds
If you are 19 or 20 years old:

- Consumption of any type of alcohol is a Class 3 Misdemeanor.

- Purchase, attempt to purchase, or possession of malt beverages or unfortified wine is a Class 3 Misdemeanor.

- Purchase, attempt to purchase, or possession of mixed beverages, spirituous liquors, or fortified wines is a Class 1 Misdemeanor.

Definitions of Types of Alcohol

- Malt beverages include beer, hard cider, and drinks such as Smirnoff Ice® and Mike's Hard Lemonade®.

- Unfortified wines include most table wines, such as Pinot Noirs, Merlots, and Chardonnays.

- Spirituous liquors include rum, vodka, gin, Jagermeister®, Rumple Minze®, and Goldschlager®.

- Fortified wines include sherry, Madeira, Marsala, port, brandy and vermouth.

❶ Pay Attention!

If you are 19 or 20 years old, you could be charged with two different classes of crimes: a Class 3 Misdemeanor for consumption of alcohol *and* a Class 1 Misdemeanor if you possess mixed beverages, spirituous liquors, or fortified wines. In any event, you can lose your license for 1 year.

❶ Pay Attention!

Even if you are not driving, a police officer may ask you to take a breathalyzer test if the police officer has probable cause to believe that you are under 21 years old and have consumed alcohol. You have a Constitutional right to refuse to consent to take a breathalyzer test. However, you need to be aware that under current North Carolina law, your refusal to consent could be used as evidence against you in court (*i.e.*, as evidence to prove you had been drinking). You also have the right to request a blood alcohol test in addition to the breathalyzer test.

❗ Pay Attention!

Note that there is no parental exception under this law. Your parent's permission does not give you the legal right to possess or consume alcohol if you are under 21 years old.

> **Example:** *P1 is under 21 years old and is watching a college football bowl game during winter break. P1's dad, P2, – thinking that all college students must be mature enough to drink alcohol – says it's okay if P1 has some beer during the game, which P1 proceeds to drink. P1 is guilty of unlawful possession and/ or consumption of alcohol, even though P1's dad, P2, gave him permission to drink. Even more, if P2 provided the beer, he could be found guilty of furnishing alcohol to persons under 21, which is also a crime, as well as aiding and abetting a crime.*

❓ Did You Know that you may be arrested if you are under 21 years old and attend a party where other people are drinking, even if you have not been drinking?

If alcohol is present and easily available for everyone at the party (including partygoers under 21 years old), the officer has probable cause to believe that any person present is in possession of alcohol and may arrest everyone under 21 years old for possession. They may also arrest you for the separate and additional crime of consumption of alcohol by a person under 21 years old. Of course, being arrested is not the same as being convicted of a crime. If you were not drinking and demanded a breathalyzer test that proved it, the court may dismiss the charge of consumption. However, under North Carolina law, you are considered guilty of possession just by having access to open alcohol, like in a keg or punch bowl.

❶ Pay Attention!

If you are under 21 years old and attend a party with alcohol and the police arrive at the party, you should request that the officer give you a breathalyzer test immediately if you have not been drinking. You may still be charged with possession if the alcohol is open and available to everyone at the party; however, you may avoid the separate and additional charge of alcohol consumption for persons under 21 years old.

Furnishing Alcohol to Persons Under 21 Years Old

A 21-year-old senior in college provided a sophomore and several of the sophomore's friends, all of whom were under 21 years old, with beer during a pre-game party in the senior's apartment. The senior did not allow anyone to drive after the party and required everyone to walk back to campus for the next party of the night. However, neighbors called the police to complain of loud noise in the complex. Police arrived at the party and discovered that persons under 21 years old had consumed alcohol given to them by the senior.

❓ Did You Know

that conviction for furnishing alcohol to persons under 21 years old can result in a 1-year revocation of your driver's license?

The senior was charged with unlawful furnishing of alcohol to minors and aiding and abetting a crime.

Crime: A crime occurs when a person provides alcoholic beverages to a person under 21 years old.

Type of Crime: Class 1 Misdemeanor

Punishment: Community punishment with up to 45 days in jail for failure to comply *and* 1-year revocation of driver's license

Exceptions:

- Licensed physicians, druggists, or dental surgeons may provide alcohol for medicinal or pharmaceutical purposes.

- An organized church or ordained minister may provide unfortified wine or fortified wine for sacramental purposes.

- An instructor at an accredited college or university may furnish alcohol to students who are under the instructor's direct supervision during a culinary class as required by established culinary curriculum.

- An employer may furnish alcohol to employees 18 to 20 years old who serve the alcohol as part of their lawful employment.

Example: *A college fraternity decides to have a keg party and serve beer. **P**, a 21 year old, goes to the liquor store and purchases the keg. If any person under 21 years old attends* *the party and consumes the beer, **P** can be charged with providing alcohol to a minor, with a separate charge for each minor, as well as aiding and abetting a crime.*

Pay Attention!

If you are 21 years old or older and host a party which may include guests under 21 years old, have partygoers identify themselves by wearing wristbands, or have a bartender who checks IDs.

Did You Know
that if you are under 21 years old and provide alcohol to someone else who is under 21 years old, you can still be charged with the crime of unlawful furnishing of alcohol to a minor? (You can also be charged as a minor in possession and with illegal consumption if you are found drinking along with your friend – making a total of 3 crimes.)

Drunk and Disorderly Conduct

Crime: The crime of drunk and disorderly conduct occurs if a person in a public place is intoxicated and disruptive in one or more of the following ways:

- Blocking or interfering with traffic on a highway or public vehicular area;

- Blocking or lying across or preventing or interfering with access to or passage across a sidewalk or entrance to a building;

- Grabbing, shoving, pushing, or fighting, or challenging others to fight;

- Cursing or shouting at or otherwise rudely insulting others; OR

- Begging for money or other property.

Type of Crime: Class 3 Misdemeanor

Punishment: Community punishment with up to 10 days in jail for failure to comply

Example: *P is intoxicated at a college sporting event and shouts obscenities at fans of the other team. P is arrested for drunk and disorderly conduct.*

Social Host Liability

A group of friends throws a housewarming party at an off-campus house. The hosts provide kegs for the guests, but they do not have a bartender and do not monitor how much the guests drink. A guest at the party proceeds to get visibly drunk and then leaves the party. While driving away from the house, the drunk guest hits another car. The driver of the car that was struck sues the friends who hosted the party and provided the keg. The friends – the party hosts and alcohol providers – may be found liable for damages caused by a guest who was known to be intoxicated and known to be driving, even if they do not know the guest.

When a host provides alcoholic beverages to another person, regardless of the person's age, the host may be found liable for damages if the host knew or reasonably should have known that the other person is intoxicated and is driving.

Chapter 10
Fake Identification and Misrepresentation of Age

Possession of Fake IDs

A college sophomore uploads her profile pic to a website that claims to make realistic-looking fake IDs. As soon as the ID arrives in her campus mailbox, she proceeds to the local ABC store. Unfortunately for the sophomore, a police officer waiting inside recognizes the student, and knows – despite what her new ID claims – that the student is not from Alaska. The sophomore will be charged with misdemeanor possession of fake identification with intent to purchase alcohol.

Sometimes college students use a fake identification document with their own photograph but false information to misrepresent their age or use another person's fake identification document. A fake identification document is one that appears to be issued – but was not actually issued – by a governmental agency or other official authority.

Crime: A crime occurs when a person under 21 years old misrepresents the person's identity or uses any false identification for the purpose of purchasing an alcoholic beverage, intending to purchase an alcoholic beverage, or being admitted to a bar.

Type of Crime: Class 1 Misdemeanor

Punishment: Community punishment with up to 45 days in jail for failure to comply *and* 1-year revocation of driver's license

Pay Attention!
While most students use fake IDs to purchase alcohol, the mere possession of a fake ID is a Class 2 Misdemeanor.

Possession of Another Person's ID

Did You Know that while it is a misdemeanor to have a fake ID, you can be charged with a felony if you use the authentic identification of another person to purchase alcohol or obtain anything of value?

A first-year student borrows a 21-year-old senior's driver's license and uses the license that Thursday night to go out to the bars. When he attempts to get into the local hotspot, the bouncer notices that the person in the picture has blue eyes, and the guy standing in front of him has brown eyes. The bouncer calls the cops, and the first-year student is arrested for using someone else's identification to obtain admission into the bar.

Crime: A crime occurs when you knowingly possess the authentic identifying information of another person to obtain anything of value.

Type of Crime: Class G Felony

Punishment: Intermediate or active punishment with a minimum of 10 months imprisonment if active punishment or for failure to comply with intermediate punishment

> **Example:** *P, who is 20 years old, obtains and uses an authentic ID of another person who is 21 years old. P is stopped by a police officer while walking back to P's apartment from a bar after having a few drinks. P hands the police officer the ID P used to get into the bar. P will be charged with a Class G Felony in addition to the crimes of underage drinking and obstruction of justice (for lying about P's identity).*

❗ Pay Attention!

Misrepresenting yourself using the ID of a real person is a felony, yet the crime of possessing alcohol as a minor is a misdemeanor.

❗ Pay Attention!

Giving your ID (whether real or fake) to another person to use for the purpose of purchasing alcohol or gaining anything of value (such as admission to a 21-year-old-and-over bar) is a misdemeanor. In addition, you could be charged with aiding and abetting and accessory before the fact. You could also lose your driver's license for 1 year.

> **Example:** *P borrows his 22-year-old brother's driver's license when P goes on spring break. When P tries to use his brother's ID to purchase liquor at the ABC store, the store clerk suspects the driver's license does not belong to P because the driver's license*

says P is 6'1", and P is clearly 5'7". The store clerk calls over an ALE officer who is on the premises, and P is arrested for identity theft. P is guilty of a Class G Felony, and the brother is guilty of a misdemeanor. Both will have their driver's licenses revoked for 1 year.

Making, Selling, or Distributing False Identification

Crime: A crime occurs when a person makes, sells, distributes, delivers, or possesses with intent to sell simulated driver's licenses as false identification documents.

Type of Crime: Class I Felony

Punishment: Community punishment with a minimum of 4 months in prison for failure to comply

Example: P finds a card printer on eBay® and purchases it for P's first-year hall. P manufactures fake IDs for all the people on the hall using their campus directory pictures. P is guilty of making and distributing false identification.

Chapter 11
Possession and Sale of Legal and Illegal Drugs

A first-year student was worried about finals because she had not done well on previous tests in the course. She heard that a drug, Adderall®, would help her focus while studying and during the test. She asked her best friend, who had a valid prescription for Adderall®, if she could have a pill to take before the final. Her friend gave her one pill from her prescription bottle. A campus police officer saw the transfer and arrested both students. The girl with the prescription was arrested for distribution of a Schedule II drug, a felony. The other girl was arrested for possession of a Schedule II drug without a valid prescription, a misdemeanor.

? Did You Know
that giving a prescription drug to a friend is a crime and that possessing a prescription drug that doesn't belong to you is a crime?

In most cases involving college students and illegal drugs, students usually know that what they are doing is against the law. However, many students do not know that *giving* a prescription drug, even just one pill, to a friend is a crime. Only pharmacists and authorized health care providers can give another person a prescription drug.

! Pay Attention!
If someone asks for your prescription pill, say *no*. Otherwise, you could be charged with a crime.

Drug Classifications

North Carolina law classifies various drugs as Schedule I, II, III, IV, V, and VI drugs, depending on whether the drug has a legitimate purpose and whether the drug can be addictive and subject to abuse. The following list describes the classification of drugs in North Carolina. This list is illustrative, not exhaustive.

- Schedule I drugs are those drugs that have no legitimate medical purpose, such as LSD, heroin, mescaline, peyote, GHB, PCP, mushrooms, and Ecstasy (E).

- Schedule II drugs are those drugs that have a medical purpose but have a high potential for abuse, such as Ritalin®, OxyContin®,

Controlled Substance Schedule

	I	II	III
Sale	Class G Felony	Class G Felony	Class H Felony
Delivery	Class H Felony	Class H Felony	Class I Felony
Manufacture	Class H Felony	Class H Felony	Class I Felony
Intent to Sell, Deliver, or Manufacture	Class H Felony	Class H Felony	Class I Felony
Possession	Class I Felony	Class 1 Misdemeanor	Class 1 Misdemeanor

Adderall®, cocaine (including crack), opium, methamphetamine (ice or crystal meth), and morphine.

• Schedule III, IV, and V drugs are those drugs that have a medical purpose but have some potential for abuse. Some common drugs are ketamine (Special K), Vicodin®, Tylenol III®, Xanax®, Librium®, Ativan®, and Rohypnol® (roofies).

• Schedule VI drugs are marijuana and its derivatives.

This chapter describes some of the laws and penalties relating to Schedule I, II, III, IV, and V drugs, and Chapter Twelve covers Schedule VI drugs (marijuana and its derivatives).

IV	V	VI	Counterfeit
Class H Felony	Class H Felony	Class H Felony	Class I Felony
Class I Felony	Class I Felony	Class I Felony	Class I Felony
Class I Felony	Class I Felony	Class I Felony	Class I Felony
Class I Felony	Class I Felony	Class I Felony	Class I Felony
Class 1 Misdemeanor	Class 2 Misdemeanor	Class 3 Misdemeanor	

Possession of Any Schedule I Drug Without a Valid Prescription

Type of Crime: Class I Felony

Punishment: Community punishment with a minimum of 4 months in prison for failure to comply

Delivery, Distribution, or Possession with Intent to Distribute Any Schedule I or II Drug

Type of crime: Class H Felony

Punishment: Community, intermediate, or active punishment with a minimum of 5 months imprisonment if active punishment or for failure to comply with community or intermediate punishment

Sale of Schedule I or II Drug

Type of Crime: Class G Felony

Punishment: Intermediate or active punishment with a minimum of 10 months imprisonment if active punishment or for failure to comply with intermediate punishment

Possession of Any Schedule II, III, IV, or V Drug Without a Valid Presciption

Type of Crime: Misdemeanor (Schedule II, III, or IV – Class 1; Schedule V – Class 2) unless the drug is methamphetamine (ice or crystal meth), amphetamine (speed), or cocaine, which is a Class I Felony.

 Punishment: See chart in Chapter Five

Delivery, Distribution, or Possession with Intent to Sell or Distribute Any Schedule III, IV, or V Drug

Type of crime: Class I Felony

Punishment: Community punishment with a minimum of 4 months in prison for failure to comply

Sale of Schedule III, IV, or V Drug

Type of Crime: Class H Felony

Punishment: Community, intermediate, or active punishment with a minimum of 5 months imprisonment if active punishment or for failure to comply with community or intermediate punishment

❗ Pay Attention!
If you are convicted of a drug-related offense while receiving federal student loans, your eligibility to receive loans may be affected.

❗ Pay Attention!
If you are 18 years old or older, you commit a Class D Felony if you sell or deliver a controlled substance to anyone 14 or 15 years old or to a pregnant female of any age. You commit a Class C Felony if you sell or deliver a controlled substance to anyone who is 13 years old or younger.

Trafficking in Cocaine

❓ Did You Know that you could be charged with trafficking in cocaine if you have 1 ounce of cocaine in your possession, even if you have no plan to sell it?

*A group of college students pools money together to purchase 1 ounce of cocaine. **P** takes the money and purchases the cocaine. **P** can be charged with trafficking in cocaine by possessing and delivering 1 ounce of cocaine.*

❓ Did You Know that you could be charged with trafficking in cocaine if you are riding in a car with an ounce of cocaine?

If several college students have the ounce of cocaine in their car when they travel to the beach for after-finals Beach Week, they can all *be charged with trafficking in cocaine for transporting it.*

📖 Crime: The crime of trafficking in cocaine occurs when a person sells, manufactures, delivers, transports, or possesses 28 grams (1 ounce) or more of cocaine.

Type of Crime: Class G Felony

Punishment: Minimum of 35 months and maximum of 42 months in prison and a minimum $50,000 fine

Pay Attention!

You can be charged with trafficking in cocaine, even if you only have possession of 1 ounce of cocaine and have no intention of selling it. The mere fact of possession is enough to charge you with a Class G Felony.

Chapter 12
Possession and Sale of Marijuana

Possession of 0.5 oz or Less of Marijuana

Type of Crime: Class 3 Misdemeanor

Punishment: Community punishment with up to 10 days in jail for failure to comply

Possession of More Than 0.5 oz but No More Than 1.5 oz of Marijuana

Type of Crime: Class 1 Misdemeanor

Punishment: Community punishment with up to 45 days in jail for failure to comply

Possession of More Than 1.5 oz of Marijuana

Type of Crime: Class I Felony

Punishment: Community punishment with a minimum of 4 months imprisonment for failure to comply

Manufacture, Sale, Delivery, or Possession with Intent to Manufacture, Sell, or Deliver Marijuana

P1 has 4 plastic bags containing a total of less than one ounce of marijuana. P1 will probably be charged with possession with intent to distribute marijuana (felony). P2, on the other hand, has one plastic bag with the same amount of marijuana. P2 may be charged only with simple possession.

Did You Know that the manner in which marijuana is packaged may determine whether the police believe marijuana is packaged for personal consumption or for distribution?

Type of Crime: Sale – Class H Felony; manufacture, delivery, or possession with intent to manufacture, sell, or deliver – Class I Felony

Punishment: Class H Felony – Community, intermediate, or active punishment with a minimum of 5 months imprisonment if active punishment or for failure to comply with community or intermediate punishment; Class I Felony – Community, intermediate, or active punishment with a minimum of 4 months imprisonment if active punishment or for failure to comply with community or intermediate punishment

Exception: The transfer of 5 grams or less of marijuana for no payment shall not constitute a delivery.

Example: *P1 freely shares a joint with P2 at a party. P1 is not guilty of "delivery" of marijuana (which would be a felony); however,*

> both *P1* and *P2* are guilty of possession of less
> than one-half ounce of marijuana (which is a
> misdemeanor).

❗ Pay Attention!
If you are convicted of a drug-related offense
while receiving federal student loans, your
eligibility to receive loans may be affected.

Chapter 13
Other Drug-Related Laws

Manufacture, Distribution, or Possession of Fake Illegal Drugs

Crime: A crime occurs when a person knowingly manufactures, distributes, or possesses with the intent to distribute anything that is alleged to be an illegal drug but is actually an imitation (such as a fake substance).

Type of Crime: Class I Felony

Punishment: Community punishment with a minimum of 4 months imprisonment for failure to comply

> **Example:** *A notorious on-campus marijuana dealer – P – supplies to P's next-door neighbor in the dorm a substance that P claims to be marijuana. In fact, it is harmless oregano P dumped out of the dispenser at a pizza place. P is nevertheless guilty of a felony.*

Asking a Person Under 18 Years Old to Deliver Illegal Drugs

A college junior asks his 15-year-old younger

sibling to deliver an ounce of marijuana for him. The sibling delivers the marijuana to the buyer. The college junior is guilty of a felony for asking his underage sibling to deliver marijuana. The younger sibling may be prosecuted in juvenile court for delivering marijuana. The buyer, if caught possessing an ounce of marijuana, is guilty of a misdemeanor.

Crime: A crime occurs when a person hires, solicits, or uses another person under 18 years old to manufacture, distribute, or deliver marijuana or other illegal drugs (including counterfeit drugs).

Type of Crime: Felony; Class depends on the age of the person hiring, the age of the minor, and the schedule of the substance

Inhalation

Crime: A crime occurs when a person intentionally smells or inhales the fumes from any substance for the purpose of inducing a condition of intoxication.

Type of Crime: Class 1 Misdemeanor

Punishment: Community punishment with up to 45 days imprisonment for failure to comply

Possession of Drug-Related Objects

Crime: A crime occurs when a person knowingly uses, or possesses with the intent to use, drug paraphernalia to:

- Plant, propagate, cultivate, grow, harvest, manufacture, compound, convert, produce, process, prepare, test, analyze, package, repackage, store, contain, or conceal a controlled substance that it would be unlawful to possess; OR

- Inject, ingest, inhale, or otherwise introduce into the body a controlled substance which it would be unlawful to possess.

Type of Crime: Class 1 Misdemeanor

Punishment: Community punishment with up to 45 days imprisonment for failure to comply

> **Example:** *P has in P's possession a bong that has been used for smoking marijuana. Even if P is not in possession of marijuana, P can be charged with a crime.*

Pay Attention!
Having drug paraphernalia on your person or in your car may give police probable cause to conduct a search.

Chapter 14
Drinking, Drugs, and Driving

? Did You Know that a person under 21 years old can be charged with driving after consuming drugs or alcohol if the person's alcohol concentration is any amount over 0.00?

? Did You Know that for most people under 21 years old, drinking only one beer or one glass of wine or one mixed drink will cause their alcohol concentration to be .02 or higher?

? Did You Know that you can be arrested for DWI if you are involved in an accident, even if the accident is not your fault?

A first-year college student attended an off-campus party with a friend and drank one beer. As he was driving with his friend to get late-night diner food, another driver ran a red light and T-boned the college student's car. Fortunately, no one was seriously injured in the accident. The police officer on the scene smelled alcohol on the college student's breath and gave him a breathalyzer test. His alcohol concentration registered .03. Although the other driver was at fault and was given a ticket for running the red light, the student was arrested and taken to jail for driving after consuming alcohol. Instead of downing a waffle and hash browns, the friend spent the rest of the night calling parents and trying to bail the guy out of county jail.

Sometimes college students are in accidents in which they are totally without fault as to the cause of the accident. However, if the officer investigating the accident smells alcohol on the student's breath, and the student registers a blood alcohol content on a breathalyzer test, the officer may arrest the student for driving after consuming alcohol, even though the alcohol was not the cause of the accident.

In North Carolina, there are two laws that may affect you if you are under 21 years old and are driving after consuming alcohol or drugs. The first is a charge of driving after consuming alcohol or drugs, which applies only to persons under 21 years old. The second is a charge of impaired driving, which applies to all drivers.

Driving After Consuming Alcohol or Drugs

Crime: The crime of driving after consuming alcohol or drugs applies to any person under 21 years old who drives a motor vehicle on any public road or highway with any amount of alcohol or a non-prescribed controlled substance remaining in the person's body.

While odor is insufficient to charge you with this crime, if the police officer has probable cause to suspect that you are guilty of this crime, the police officer may require you to submit to a drug or alcohol screening test. If you refuse to take the test, your refusal can be used against you, and your license will be immediately revoked. You also have the right to request a blood alcohol test in addition to the breathalyzer test.

Type of Crime: Class 2 Misdemeanor

Punishment: Community punishment with up to 30 days in jail for failure to comply *and* 1-year revocation of your driver's license

Example: *P is 18 years old and consents to a breathalyzer test. The test shows an alcohol concentration of .02. P is guilty of driving after consuming alcohol, a Class 2 Misdemeanor, and will have his license revoked for 1 year.*

Impaired Driving (DWI)

A 21-year-old student is driving her hall mates to the 24-hour grocery store for a late-night ice cream and candy binge after a costume party. The student consumed beer from six full red plastic cups while at the party. While driving, she is stopped by a police officer – while still wearing a twin extra-long sheet pinned together as a toga – and charged with driving after consuming alcohol and impaired driving because her blood alcohol content was .09. The student is arrested for impaired driving and taken to jail in her toga, where she will spend the rest of the weekend before her parents can bail her out.

Crime: The crime of impaired driving occurs when a person drives a motorized vehicle upon any highway, street, or public vehicular area under any of the following conditions:

- Under the influence of an impairing substance;

- With an alcohol concentration of .08 or more at any relevant time after driving a vehicle; OR

- Under the influence of any amount of a Schedule I controlled substance.

Type of Crime: Misdemeanor

Punishment: Up to a $200 fine and between 24 hours and 60 days in jail, which may be suspended and served by doing community service

Exception: There is an important exception to this general rule. If you are convicted of impaired driving, and you have a passenger in your car who is under 16 years old, or you cause serious injury to another person, your punishment will be a minimum of 7 days in jail and a maximum of 12 months in jail and a maximum fine of $2,000. Some courts have ruled that each passenger in your car under 16 constitutes a separate violation.

Pay Attention!
You can also be charged for DWI when driving a boat, a jet ski, a lawnmower, or any motorized vehicle, or when riding a bicycle or waterskiing.

Implied Consent and the Breathalyzer Test

If a police officer has probable cause and arrests you for impaired driving or driving after consuming alcohol or drugs, the officer is required to ask you whether you are willing to consent to a breathalyzer or blood alcohol test. If you have a driver's license, you have essentially given your implied consent to a breathalyzer or blood alcohol test in exchange for the privilege of driving. However, every person, even those under 21 years old, has the right to refuse the test. Note, though, that if you refuse the test, your driver's license will automatically be suspended for 12 months. Further, the fact that you refused the test can later be used against you at a trial for driving under the influence.

The following charts approximate blood alcohol content for males and females based on body weight and number of drinks consumed in a 1-hour period. However, a number of other factors may

Blood Alcohol Percentage Level Chart for Males

Body Weight	Number of Drinks Consumed in One Hour				
	1	2	3	4	5
100 lbs	.04	.08	.11	.15	.19
120 lbs	.03	.06	.09	.12	.16
140 lbs	.03	.05	.08	.11	.13
160 lbs	.02	.05	.07	.09	.12
180 lbs	.02	.04	.06	.08	.11
200 lbs	.02	.04	.06	.08	.09

affect your blood alcohol content, such as your age, metabolism, medications, speed of consumption, health issues, and the amount of food in your stomach and small intestine. In the calculation below, one drink is equivalent to one 12 oz. regular beer, 5 oz. of wine, or a 1.5 oz. shot of hard liquor.

There is no "safe" amount to drink and still be able to drive without impairment. Any amount of alcohol meets the driving after consuming alcohol standard for persons under 21 years old in North Carolina.

Blood Alcohol Percentage Level Chart for Females

Body Weight	Number of Drinks Consumed in One Hour				
	1	2	3	4	5
90 lbs	.05	.10	.15	.20	.25
100 lbs	.05	.09	.14	.18	.23
120 lbs	.04	.08	.11	.15	.19
140 lbs	.03	.07	.10	.13	.16
160 lbs	.03	.06	.09	.11	.14
180 lbs	.03	.05	.08	.10	.13

❶ Pay Attention!
The best rule to follow is don't ever drink and drive, and certainly don't drive if you're under 21 years old and have had *anything* to drink. The legal consequences are just too devastating.

Open Container Violation

❓ Did You Know that a violation of the open container law occurs even if no one in the car has been drinking?

A student is stopped by the police for speeding. The officer sees a bottle of bourbon in the passenger seat that has a broken seal. Even though it is 10 a.m. on a Sunday and the driver has not been drinking, the student and all passengers can be charged with an open container violation.

📖 Crime: A crime occurs when a driver or passenger of a motor vehicle possesses or has ready access to an open container of alcohol.

An open container of alcohol means any open can or bottle or a bottle that has a broken seal or has the contents partially removed.

All that is required is that the driver or passenger has access to an open container of alcohol. No one in the car has to be drinking.

Your car does not have to be in motion; you can be charged if your car is parked and running in a parking lot, such as a parking lot at a school, college, university, apartment building, office building, supermarket, or store.

Type of Crime: Class 3 Misdemeanor

Punishment: Community punishment with up to 10 days in jail for failure to comply

Pay Attention!

Even designated drivers who are not drinking can be charged with open container violations if they allow anyone to ride in the car with an open container of alcohol.

V. Sex and Sexual Exploitation

Chapter 15
Sex Crimes with Force

Rape

An 18-year-old first-year student went to a fraternity party, where she had a significant amount of alcohol. She blacked out later that evening, but she awoke the next morning in someone else's bed, unclothed and feeling sick, with a guy next to her whom she did not remember. She could tell that at some point she had had sex the night before, but she did not remember doing it. She went back to her dorm and told her roommate, and they went to a rape crisis clinic, where she told her story to a counselor. The police were called, and the boy she found in bed with her was arrested for second-degree rape.

? Did You Know that you commit rape if you have sex with someone who is too intoxicated to give her consent?

North Carolina has two degrees of rape, as explained below.

Both males and females can be convicted of the crime of rape.

Rape involves **sexual intercourse**, which means vaginal intercourse.

Second-Degree Rape

 **Crime:** The crime of second-degree rape occurs when a person forces another person to have sexual intercourse against the other person's will or a person has sexual intercourse with another person who is mentally disabled, mentally incapacitated, or physically helpless, and the person has reason to know of the incapacitation.

For second-degree rape, force does not require a weapon. Force does not require actual physical injury to the female. Fear and intimidation may be all that is necessary to show force.

Type of Crime: Class C Felony

Punishment: Minimum of 58 months imprisonment

First-Degree Rape

Crime: The crime of first-degree rape occurs when a person forces another person to have sexual intercourse against the other person's will and employs a deadly weapon, inflicts serious physical injury, or is aided by a third party.

Example: P1 decides to have sexual intercourse with V. V states that she does not wish to have sex with P1. P1's friend, P2, is in the room and holds down V while P1 and V have non-consensual intercourse. P1 is guilty of first-degree rape. P2 is also guilty of aiding and abetting rape.

Type of Crime: Class B1 Felony

Punishment: Minimum of 16 years imprisonment

Pay Attention!
"Against the will of another person" does not require the person to say "no." The person can show refusal by any means necessary to show he or she does not want to engage in sexual intercourse.

Pay Attention!
If an individual is so intoxicated by alcohol or drugs that the individual is incapable of giving consent, then the elements of "force" and "against the will of another person" are assumed to be proven.

Pay Attention!
Most victims of rape know the person who commits the rape. Often, consensual interactions precede rape – for example, hooking up without intercourse or dancing closely at a party. Rape under these circumstances is sometimes called "date rape."

Pay Attention!
The fact that a victim consents to romantic acts leading up to forced intercourse is *not* a defense for rape. A person must explicitly, while not under the influence of alcohol or drugs, consent to vaginal intercourse for the intercourse to be considered consensual.

❗ Pay Attention!

If a person puts a controlled substance (such as roofies) into another person's food or drink to make the other person become mentally or physically helpless with the intent of committing rape or a sexual offense, the person will be guilty of a Class G Felony for putting the controlled substance into the person's food or drink.

> **Example:** *Unknown to V, P gives V a drink laced with a sedative known commonly as the "Date Rape" drug. V does not remember anything that happened after she had the drink but finds herself in bed the next morning with P and realizes that she has had sex the night before. V goes immediately to a rape crisis clinic and tests positive for roofies. P will be charged with second-degree rape and with the additional crime of contaminating another's drink to render the person helpless (putting roofies in V's drink).*

❗ Pay Attention!

If you believe you have been a victim of rape, do not bathe or wash your clothes (otherwise, you may compromise evidence of the rape). Report the rape immediately to the police or a rape crisis center.

Sexual Offense

A guy and a girl are grinding on the dance floor at a party. The room is dark, the night's getting late, and the two are making out. The guy decides to make a bold move and insert his finger into his dance partner's vagina. The girl pulls back, yet the guy continues to push and uses force to insert his finger into the girl's vagina without her consent. The guy is guilty of second-degree sexual offense.

North Carolina has two degrees of sexual offense, as explained below.

Borh males and females can be convicted of the crime of sexual offense.

Sexual offense involves a **sexual act**, which means oral sex, anal sex, and any penetration other than vaginal intercourse, however slight, by any object into the genital or anal opening of another person's body.

Second-Degree Sexual Offense

Crime: The crime of second-degree sexual offense occurs when a person engages in a sexual act with another person against the other person's will and by the use of force or a person engages in a sexual act with another person who is mentally disabled, mentally incapacitated, or physically helpless, and the person has reason to know of the incapacitation.

Type of Crime: Class C Felony

Punishment: Minimum of 58 months imprisonment

First-Degree Sexual Offense

Crime: The crime of first-degree sexual offense occurs when a person engages in a sexual act with another person against the other person's will and by the use of force and employs a deadly weapon, inflicts serious physical injury, or is assisted by one or more other people.

Type of Crime: Class B1 Felony

Punishment: Minimum of 16 years imprisonment

Sexual Battery

Did You Know that you can be charged with sexual battery for touching your girlfriend's breasts after she says no?

*Banished from their rooms by roommates who are studying for exams, **P** is making out with his girlfriend in the rear seat of his car in the back of a student parking lot. **P** grabs his girlfriend's breast and she tells him to stop. He continues to massage her breasts. **P** can be charged with sexual battery.*

Crime: The crime of sexual battery occurs when a person touches the genital area, groin, anus, buttocks, or breast with force and against the other person's will for the purpose of sexual arousal, sexual gratification, or sexual abuse.

Touching outer clothing in these areas can be sexual battery; skin contact is not required.

Sexual battery is gender-neutral. A male or a female can be a victim or a perpetrator of sexual battery.

Type of Crime: Class A1 Misdemeanor

Punishment: Community, intermediate, or active punishment with up to 60 days in jail for active punishment or for failure to comply with community or intermediate punishment

Sex Offender Registry

If you are convicted as an adult for a sexually violent offense, including sexual battery, you will be required to register as a sex offender. Other convictions that require registering for the sex offender registry include a) sex-related offenses against minors (including "sexting") (see Chapter Sixteen); b) aiding and abetting sex-related offenses against minors or sexually violent offenses (see Chapter Four); and c) secretly peeping (see Chapter Eighteen). Registration can be for as long as 30 years. The sex offender registry is a public record. Being listed on the sex offender registry has drastic negative consequences and dictates limited options for employment and where you can live.

Chapter 16
Sexting and Sexual Exploitation of Minors

You may be thinking, "I would *never* commit a crime as outrageous as sexual exploitation of minors!" Before you skip to the next chapter, hold up: this crime is more common than you think. You or someone you know may have committed a crime of sexual exploitation, such as "sexting." And the consequences are severe: not only is sexual exploitation of a minor a felony, but a person convicted of this crime must register on the sex offender registry, which has a devastating and long-lasting impact (see Chapter Fifteen).

? Did You Know that if you take sexually explicit photographs or videos of a person under 18 years old – including yourself – you commit a felony?

An 18-year-old first-year student, home from college for Thanksgiving break, went to the home of his 17-year-old girlfriend, a high school senior. No one else was home, and the excited couple went upstairs to her bedroom, where they made a video of the two of them performing various sexual acts. In the ecstasy of the moment, they misplaced the video. The girl's little sister found the video and, thoroughly confused, gave it to her parents. The boy was arrested for first-degree and second-degree sexual exploitation of a minor; the girl was arrested for second-degree exploitation of a minor. Both first-degree and second-degree sexual exploitation of minors are felonies.

First-Degree Sexual Exploitation of a Minor

Crime: The crime of first-degree sexual exploitation of a minor (anyone under 18 years old) occurs when a person encourages or facilitates a minor to engage in sexual activity for the purpose of producing material that contains a visual representation (such as a picture or a video) of this activity.

Type of Crime: Class C Felony

Punishment: Active punishment with a minimum of 58 months imprisonment

Example: *A college sophomore, P, goes on Spring Break to Myrtle Beach. P hooks up with V, whom P thinks is 18 years old. P convinces V that they should videotape their hook-up to commemorate the vacation. Turns out, V lied and is actually 17 years old and a senior at the local high school. P is guilty of a felony, first-degree sexual exploitation of a minor.*

Pay Attention!
Sexual exploitation of a minor is a felony, regardless of your age, *even if you are the same age*. The crime is also gender-neutral. The fact that both parties consented to the activity does not matter.

Second-Degree Sexual Exploitation of a Minor

A 17-year-old girl, a senior in high school, takes a picture with her cell phone showing herself masturbating and sends it to her boyfriend, who is away at college. After a fight about their long-distance relationship, he sends the picture to some of his friends. The college student and his (ex-)girlfriend are both charged with second-degree sexual exploitation of a minor: the college student for distributing material that contains a visual representation of a minor engaged in sexual activity, and the high school student for making and distributing material that contains a visual representation of a minor engaged in sexual activity.

Crime: The crime of second-degree sexual exploitation of a minor (anyone under 18 years old) occurs when a person, knowing the character or content of the material:

- Records, photographs, films, develops, or duplicates material that contains a visual representation of a minor engaged in sexual activity; OR

- Distributes, transports, exhibits, receives, sells, purchases, exchanges, or solicits material that contains a visual representation of a minor engaged in sexual activity.

This crime is commonly referred to as **sexting**.

Type of Crime: Class E Felony

Punishment: Intermediate or active punishment with a minimum of 20 months imprisonment for active punishment or failure to comply with intermediate punishment

Third-Degree Sexual Exploitation of a Minor

A 16-year-old girl takes a cell phone video of herself performing oral sex on her new boyfriend. She sends it to her ex-boyfriend – who is now off at college playing football – to make him jealous. The ex-boyfriend sends it to the entire football team. The girl is guilty of second-degree sexual exploitation, for recording and sending the video to her ex-boyfriend. The ex-boyfriend is guilty of second-degree sexual exploitation, for sending the video to the football team. Those members of the football team who do not delete the video from their phones are guilty of third-degree sexual exploitation for possessing the video.

Did You Know that if you possess sexually explicit material featuring minors in electronic storage – such as an e-mail account, a photo-sharing page, a downloaded shared file – even if it is in the electronic "trash," you may be guilty of third-degree sexual exploitation of a minor?

Crime: The crime of third-degree sexual exploitation of a minor (anyone under 18 years old) occurs when a person, knowing the character or content of the material, possesses material that contains a visual representation of a minor engaging in sexual activity.

Type of Crime: Class H Felony

Punishment: Community, intermediate, or active punishment with a minimum of 5 months imprisonment for active punishment or failure to comply with community or intermediate punishment

Pay Attention!

The best rule of thumb is not to take or allow others to take sexually explicit pictures or videos of you and immediately delete anything you receive. Such pictures could end up on a social networking site and could come back to haunt you later when applying to graduate school or for jobs.

Chapter 17
Age of Consent and Statutory Rape

A 20-year-old male college honor student met the female cousin of one of his neighbors when he was home for summer vacation. The cousin was staying in town for several weeks. She told the boy she was 17 years old. He had no reason not to believe her because she looked 17, and she was in high school. (She was actually only 15 years old.) They dated several times during the summer and had sexual intercourse.

When her vacation ended and school started, the girl went back to her home and her (sophomore year of) high school, and the boy started his junior year of college. One morning, the girl's mother accidentally found her daughter's diary and read all about her daughter's summer romance. (Let's just say it was a very detailed account, too much information by most standards.) The mother told her husband, and they both drove to the town where their daughter had spent the summer and got a judge to issue a warrant for the boy's arrest for statutory rape. He was taken out of his lecture, arrested, and taken off to jail in handcuffs, where he was locked up with the other adult prisoners.

Even though the boy reasonably believed his girlfriend was over 16, he was still guilty of statutory rape because she was actually only 15 at

? Did You Know that you can be charged with statutory rape, even if the other person tells you he or she is 16 years old?

? Did You Know that you can be charged with statutory rape, even if the other person under 16 years old consents to have sex?

the time they had sex.

Crime: The crime of sexual offense of a person 13, 14, or 15 years old occurs when a person has sexual intercourse or engages in a sexual act with a person who is 13, 14, or 15 years old, IF the person committing the crime is more than 4 years older than the person who is 13, 14, or 15 years old.

This crime is sometimes called **statutory rape**.

The age difference between the parties is determined based on each person's birth date.

Sexual intercourse means vaginal intercourse. **Sexual act** means oral sex, anal sex, and any other penetration (except for vaginal intercourse), however slight, by any object into the genital or anal opening of another person's body.

Type of Crime: If more than 4 years but less than 6 years older than the victim – Class C Felony; if at least 6 years older than the victim – Class B1 Felony

Punishment: Class C Felony – minimum of 58 months imprisonment; Class B1 Felony – minimum of 16 years imprisonment

Did You Know that you can be charged with statutory rape regardless of whether you are a girl or a boy?

Statutory rape is gender-neutral. A male or a female can be either a victim or a perpetrator of statutory rape. Consent (permission and willingness) to sexual intercourse or a sexual act is irrelevant.

Example: *P, a female, is 20 years old, and V is 15 years old. P and V have sexual intercourse. Because P is more than 4 years but less than 6 years older than V, P is guilty of statutory rape (Class C Felony), with punishment of a minimum of 58 months imprisonment.*

Chapter 18
Other Sex Crimes

Indecent Exposure

A guy dropped his shorts to his ankles and mooned a woman in the apartment building next door. Even though the woman only saw his buttocks, because his pants were around his ankles and he was wearing nothing other than his running shoes and a baseball hat, he had in fact willfully exposed his private parts in a public place in the presence of a member of the opposite sex. The guy is guilty of indecent exposure, regardless of whether the woman saw his private parts or not.

Crime: The crime of indecent exposure occurs when a person willfully exposes his or her private parts in a public place in the presence of a member of the opposite sex.

Showing *only* your buttocks is not a crime.

A public place can be in the privacy of one's own home or backyard if it is reasonable to expect that someone on the outside has a view of the home or backyard.

Type of Crime: Class 2 Misdemeanor

Punishment: Community punishment with up to 30 days in jail for failure to comply

Example: *P is dared by her friends to streak across the front main lawn of campus during broad daylight. P strips down and streaks naked, where a male professor sees P while he is walking to class. The professor calls the police, and P is arrested for indecent exposure.*

Secretly Peeping into Room Occupied by Another Person

Crime: A crime occurs when a person peeps secretly into any room occupied by another person

Type of Crime: Class 1 Misdemeanor

Exception: If a person, while secretly peeping into any room, uses any device to create a photographic image of another person in that room for the purpose of arousing or gratifying the sexual desire of any person, the person is guilty of a Class I Felony.

Punishment: Class 1 Misdemeanor – Community punishment with up to 45 days in jail for failure to comply; Class I Felony – Community punishment with a minimum of 4 months imprisonment for failure to comply and registration on the sex offender registry (see Chapter Fifteen)

VI. Safety and Injury: Threats and Bodily Harm to You and Others

Chapter 19
Threats to Safety and Bodily Harm

Chapter 20
Taking Another Person's Life

Chapter 21
Self-Defense

Chapter 22
Weapons and Firearms

Chapter 19
Threats to Safety and Bodily Harm

College students get into trouble with crimes such as assault and battery primarily for three reasons: 1) they are intoxicated; 2) they lose their temper and do not think about the consequences of their actions; or 3) they are goaded by their friends into doing something stupid, such as firing a gun at someone's house.

Remember: "My fraternity brothers made me do it!" is not a defense for committing a crime.

Assault and Battery

Following a party in his room, a student believed that a guy down the hall had stolen his iPod. The student knocked on the guy's door, and when he opened it, the student raised his fist and told the guy to return his iPod, or he was going to hit him. Although the student never hit him, the student was still guilty of assault because he threatened the guy with a violent injury.

Did You Know that threatening someone with violence might be enough to charge you with assault?

Crime: The crime of assault or assault and battery occurs when a person:

• Intentionally offers or attempts by force or violence to do injury to another person; AND

• Shows violence causing a reasonable person to fear immediate bodily harm.

❶ Pay Attention!

The aggressor does not actually have to harm the other person. A crime occurs if the other person reasonably believes harm is about to happen.

Type of Crime: Class 2 Misdemeanor

⚖ Punishment:

Community punishment with up to 30 days in jail for failure to comply

Exception: An assault or assault and battery is a more serious Class 1 Misdemeanor if it is against a sports official, such as an umpire or referee.

> **Example:** *P has a strike called against her during an intramural softball game, which she believes should have been called a ball. In anger, P raises her fist to the umpire and says, "I'll show you a strike, when I strike you with my fist!" P is guilty of assault, a Class 1 Misdemeanor.*

Exception: An assault or assault and battery is a Class A1 Misdemeanor if it inflicts serious injury upon another, involves the use of a deadly weapon, OR is on a child under 12 years old, a police officer, a state official, a school official or volunteer, or a female (if the male perpetrator is at least 18 years old).

Serious injury is physical injury that causes great pain and suffering.

> **Example:** *P, who is drunk and angry at V for hooking up with her ex-boyfriend at a party, grabs a softball bat (a deadly weapon) from her dorm room and chases after V, but never catches her. P is guilty of assault, as a Class A1 Misdemeanor.*

Felonious Assault

There are several circumstances when assault is a felony, depending on whether and what type of injury results and whether deadly weapons are used.

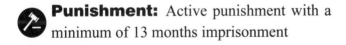

Crime: The crime of assault is a felony if a person commits an assault and causes serious bodily injury.

Serious bodily injury includes injury that causes a coma or permanent damage to a body part or organ.

Type of Crime: Class F Felony

Punishment: Active punishment with a minimum of 13 months imprisonment

> **Example:** *P and V engage in a fistfight. P strikes a blow to V's head, which results in permanent brain damage. P has committed felonious assault, a Class F Felony.*

Crime: The crime of assault is a felony if a person commits an assault with a deadly weapon with intent to kill, and serious injury results.

Serious injury is physical injury that causes great pain and suffering.

Type of Crime: Class C Felony

Punishment: Active punishment with a minimum of 58 months imprisonment

> **Example:** *P and V engage in a fight. P has a knife and tries to kill V by stabbing V in the heart. V survives but suffers serious injury. P has committed assault, a Class C Felony.*

Crime: The crime of assault is a felony if a person commits an assault with a deadly weapon (but without intent to kill), and serious injury results.

Type of Crime: Class E Felony

Punishment: Active punishment with a minimum of 20 months imprisonment

> **Example:** *P and V engage in a fight. P has a knife and stabs V in the leg, causing serious injury to V. P has committed assault, a Class E Felony.*

Crime: The crime of assault is a felony if a person commits an assault with a deadly weapon with intent to kill but doesn't cause any injury to the other person.

Type of Crime: Class E Felony

Punishment: Active punishment with a minimum of 20 months imprisonment

> **Example:** *P and V engage in a fight. P has a gun and tries to shoot V in the chest but misses. P has committed assault, a Class E Felony.*

Resisting Officers

Crime: The crime of resisting officers occurs when any person willfully and unlawfully resists, delays, or obstructs a public officer in discharging or attempting to discharge the officer's official duties.

Type of Crime: Class 2 Misdemeanor

Punishment: Community punishment with up to 30 days in jail for failure to comply

> **Example:** *A police officer arrives at a party where there is underage drinking and approaches P for questioning. P starts to run from the officer instead of answering any questions. P is guilty of resisting officers by obstruction of a police officer.*

Example: *P sees a police officer approach from across the street. P, who is under 21 years old, has been drinking and is walking down the sidewalk on the way home from a bar. The officer asks P for P's ID. P hands the officer P's fake ID, which says P is over 21. The officer recognizes that the ID is a fake and arrests P for the crime of resisting officers in addition to crimes related to underage drinking and possession and use of a fake ID.*

Communicating Threats

Did You Know that it is a crime to threaten to do violence against another person if communicated to that person?

Two college students were having a dispute over a girl. One of the boys called the other boy and left a voice message stating, "If you don't quit messin' with my girl, I'm gonna kill you!" He was arrested for communicating threats.

Crime: The crime of communicating threats is committed when a person willfully threatens to injure physically another person, another person's child, sibling, or spouse or willfully threatens to damage another person's property by communicating the threat to the other person, and a reasonable person would believe that the threat is likely to be carried out.

Type of Crime: Class 1 Misdemeanor

Punishment: Community punishment with up to 45 days in jail for failure to comply

> **Example:** *P finds out that V asked his girlfriend out on a date. P threatens to slash V's tires if V ever talks to P's girlfriend again. P is guilty of communicating threats.*

Stalking

An 18-year-old first-year college student broke up with his high school girlfriend while he was away at school. When he came home for spring break, his former girlfriend started harassing him by leaving numerous voicemails on his cell phone. She also parked her car in front of his home. He asked her to leave him alone, to stop leaving him phone messages, and not to follow him. One evening he came home with a date, and his former girlfriend jumped from the bushes and attacked his date with a purse. She was arrested for stalking and battery.

Crime: The crime of stalking occurs when a person willfully on more than one occasion harasses another person or engages in a course of conduct that would cause a reasonable person to fear for the person's safety or suffer substantial emotional distress.

Type of Crime: Class A1 Misdemeanor

Punishment: Community, intermediate, or active punishment with up to 60 days in jail for active punishment or for failure to comply with community or intermediate punishment

❶ Pay Attention!
If you believe you are a victim of stalking, immediately tell your parents or a trusted adult. If the stalker does not stop the behavior, notify the police immediately before someone gets physically injured.

Cyberstalking

❓ Did You Know that it is a crime to text another person repeatedly for the purpose of annoying the person?

A girl breaks up with her boyfriend. He is upset and text messages his now-ex-girlfriend 45 times in one evening asking, "Why??????" The ex-boyfriend is guilty of cyberstalking.

📖 Crime: The crime of cyberstalking occurs when a person, via electronic mail or communication, including text messaging:

- Threatens to inflict bodily harm to another or another's children, sibling, spouse, or dependent or physical injury to their property;

- Repeatedly communicates with another to abuse, annoy, threaten, terrify, harass, or embarrass the other person; OR

- Communicates false statements concerning death, injury, illness, indecent conduct or criminal conduct of another person or their family with the intent to abuse, annoy, threaten, terrify, harass, or embarrass.

Type of Crime: Class 2 Misdemeanor

⚖ Punishment: Community punishment with up to 30 days in jail for failure to comply

False Imprisonment

Following rush week, a sorority hosts a get-to-know-us night with its new pledges. The sisters start a drinking version of Never Have I Ever. One of the pledges becomes uncomfortable and asks to leave. One of the sisters locks the door of the room and says, "You're not allowed to leave; this is mandatory!" Now the pledge really wants to leave, yet she is confined to the room and the Never Have I Ever game without her consent. The sister who locked the door is guilty of false imprisonment, a Class 1 Misdemeanor.

Crime: The crime of false imprisonment occurs when one person confines or restrains another person without the other person's consent.

Type of Crime: Class 1 Misdemeanor

Punishment: Community punishment with up to 45 days in jail for failure to comply

Felonious Restraint

Crime: The crime of felonious restraint occurs when one person confines or restrains another person without the person's consent and then moves the restrained person from the place of initial restraint (usually by vehicle).

Type of Crime: Class F Felony

Punishment: Intermediate or active punishment with a minimum of 13 months imprisonment for active punishment or for failure to comply with intermediate punishment

> **Example:** *P blindfolds V as part of a game and leads V into P's car. P announces to V that they will travel to another city and be gone for the rest of the night. V objects and asks to get out of the car because V wants to go to another party. P ignores V and starts driving. P is guilty of felonious restraint.*

Chapter 20
Taking Another Person's Life

All of us know that intentionally killing another person is murder and is against the law. However, the law breaks down homicide – taking another person's life – into categories other than murder and covers situations that unfortunately may arise among college students.

Involuntary Manslaughter

Crime: The crime of involuntary manslaughter occurs when a person kills another human being without intent or malice. This crime can result from an unlawful act or an act done negligently or from failing to act.

Type of crime: Class F Felony

Punishment: Intermediate or active punishment with a minimum of 13 months imprisonment for active punishment or for failure to comply with intermediate punishment.

Pay Attention!
Involuntary manslaughter is the most likely type of homicide that may occur among college students. There are many reckless things college students can do that can result in the death of

another person. Such deaths are tragic for all parties involved. If someone dies, and you acted negligently or failed to act responsibly, you may be found criminally liable for that person's death.

> **Example:** *P and V go to a party together. V proceeds to do 20 tequila shots. P drives V home, and V passes out in P's car. When P arrives at V's apartment, P drags V out of the car and leaves V on the steps to the apartment without a jacket in below freezing temperature. P drives away. V dies of hypothermia. P may be charged with involuntary manslaughter.*

> **Example:** *V is not feeling well, and P offers V some prescription antibiotic drugs that P had been given previously for an infection but had not taken. Several days later, V has an allergic reaction to the medication and becomes very ill. P gets nervous and concerned about her friend, though P is scared she will get in trouble for giving V the medication. P convinces herself V will be okay, and P does not call for medical help even though V requests assistance. When V becomes unconscious, P finally calls 911. V's kidneys fail, and V dies. P may be charged with involuntary manslaughter.*

Voluntary Manslaughter

Crime: The crime of voluntary manslaughter occurs when a person kills a human being without premeditation and deliberation, without malice, and without the intention to kill or to inflict serious bodily injury.

To be found guilty of voluntary manslaughter instead of murder in the first degree, the defendant must act in the heat of passion and be seriously provoked by the victim.

Mere words or name-calling by the other person cannot be enough to provoke someone to commit voluntary manslaughter.

If there is a "cooling off" period between the time of being provoked and the killing, the crime will be murder instead of voluntary manslaughter.

Type of crime: Class D Felony

 Punishment: Active punishment with a minimum of 51 months imprisonment

> **Example:** *P finds his best friend, V, dancing on a table and making out with P's girlfriend. In a rage, P grabs a bat, jumps on the table, and hits V with the bat. V dies from an injury to his head. P may be guilty of voluntary manslaughter instead of murder.*

> **Example:** *P finds his best friend, V, dancing on a table and making out with P's girlfriend. Several hours later, P beats V with a bat while V is sleeping. P may be guilty of murder, a Class A Felony (punishable by life imprisonment*

without parole and the possibility of the death penalty), not voluntary manslaughter.

Felony Murder

A girl, heartbroken and angry over being dropped by her longtime boyfriend, goes to his apartment in the middle of the night. She pours lighter fluid on a sofa on the porch outside his door. She sets it on fire, rings her ex-boyfriend's doorbell, and runs away. The boyfriend unfortunately is fast asleep and does not hear the doorbell. The sofa continues to burn, eventually catching the apartment building on fire. Four tenants, asleep in their apartments, die of smoke inhalation.

Crime: The crime of felony murder occurs when a person takes the life of another during the commission of certain felonies (arson, rape or sexual offense, robbery, kidnapping, and burglary) or any other felony committed or attempted with the use of a deadly weapon.

A person can be convicted of felony murder even if the person never intended to kill anyone.

Type of Crime: Class A Felony

Punishment: Active punishment with a minimum of life imprisonment without parole and the possibility of the death penalty

Chapter 21
Self-Defense

People often ask when self-defense is appropriate and what kind of self-defense is legal. Our first advice is to try to avoid the issue. If at all possible, remove yourself from the situation. There are worse things than being called a coward – such as going to prison or dying.

Self-defense may be a legal defense for certain crimes.

If a person uses force or threatens to use force against you, you may use self-defense if you reasonably believe that force, and the degree of force that you use, is necessary to defend yourself or a third person from immediate harm.

You may only use deadly force or force that is likely to cause serious bodily injury if you reasonably believe that such force is necessary to prevent death or serious bodily injury to yourself or a third person. Deadly force or force that may cause serious bodily injury is also permissible to prevent a forcible felony. A person is not required to retreat before using force to defend the person or a third person.

Example: *P stops V on the street to ask for the time, then proceeds to threaten V with a knife. V reasonably believes that P is about* *to kill or seriously injure V. V may use self-defense as V's defense if V kills or seriously injures P to prevent injury to V.*

Example: *P is forcibly trying to have sex with V against V's will. V believes that P is about to rape V. V may use self-defense as a defense if V kills or seriously injures P.*

Exceptions: In some situations, self-defense will not be a valid legal defense for using force against another person. You may not use force:

• If you are the initial aggressor or were engaged in a fight by mutual agreement; OR

• If you provoke force against another person with the intent of inflicting bodily harm.

Example: *P picks a fight with V. When V retaliates, P uses force against V, which causes V to have a broken nose. The instigator – P – cannot use self-defense as a defense for P's actions.*

❗ Pay Attention!
If the original threat is no longer a threat, then your actions are no longer self-defense. That is to say, if a person punches you and you punch the person back and knock the person out, you are not acting in self-defense if you proceed to kick the person.

❗ Pay Attention!

Self-defense will also not be a valid legal defense if you use force to protect your belongings, such as your car or your backpack.

> **Example:** *P1 sees P2 spray-painting P1's car, and P1 proceeds to beat up P2. P1 may not claim self-defense as a defense for the crime of assault.*

Chapter 22
Weapons and Firearms

Possession of a Weapon on Campus or Other Educational Property

A college student goes on a hunting trip over the weekend and leaves a rifle in the trunk of the student's car. The student drives back to campus on Sunday afternoon, without returning the gun to the student's parents' house. The Resident Advisor on the hall overhears the student telling a hall mate about the weekend of hunting and that the gun is still in the trunk of the student's car. The Resident Advisor reports the incident to the campus police, who search the student's car and find the gun. The student is charged with a Class G Felony for having a weapon – and a weapon that is a firearm – on campus.

Crime: A felony occurs when a person possesses or carries, whether openly or concealed, any gun, rifle, pistol, or other firearm of any kind, as well as any dynamite cartridge, bomb, grenade, mine, or powerful explosive, on educational property or to an academic or extracurricular activity sponsored by a college.

Crime: A misdemeanor occurs when a person possesses or carries, whether openly or concealed, any BB gun, stun gun, air rifle, air pistol, bowie knife, dirk, dagger, slungshot, leaded cane, switchblade knife, blackjack, metallic knuckles, razors and razor blades (except solely for personal shaving), firework, or any sharp-pointed or edged instrument except instructional supplies, unaltered nail files and clips and tools used solely for preparation of food, instruction, and maintenance, on educational property.

Educational property includes any school building or vehicle, school campus, grounds, recreational area, athletic field, or other property owned, used, or operated by any board of education or school board of trustees, or directors for the administration of any school.

Type of Crime: Felony possession – Class G Felony; Misdemeanor possession – Class 1 Misdemeanor

Punishment: Class G Felony – Intermediate or active punishment with a minimum of 10 months imprisonment for active punishment or for failure to comply with intermediate punishment; Class 1 Misdemeanor – Community punishment with up to 45 days for failure to comply

Pay Attention!
The fact that the weapon or explosive device is locked in a person's vehicle is insignificant; possession in any location on educational property is a crime.

Possession of a Handgun without a License

Crime: A crime occurs when a person carries a concealed handgun without a concealed handgun permit, unless the person is on the person's own premises or is allowed as a member of the military.

Type of Crime: Class 2 Misdemeanor

Punishment: Community punishment with up to 30 days in jail for failure to comply

Selling or Furnishing a Handgun to a Person Under 18 Years Old

Crime: A crime occurs when a person sells, offers for sale, gives, or in any way transfers to a minor (person under 18 years old) any handgun.

Exception: A crime does not occur if the handgun is loaned to a minor for temporary use if the minor's possession of the handgun is for lawful purposes, such as a) possessing a handgun for educational or recreational purposes while the minor is supervised by an adult who is present, or b) possessing a handgun while hunting or trapping outside the limits of an incorporated municipality if the minor has written permission from a parent or guardian.

Type of Crime: Class H Felony

Punishment: Community, intermediate, or active punishment with a minimum of 5 months imprisonment for active punishment or for failure to comply with community or intermediate punishment

Carrying Concealed Weapons Other Than Handguns

Crime: A crime occurs when any person willfully and intentionally carries such deadly weapons as a bowie knife, dirk, dagger, slungshot, loaded crane, metallic knuckles, razor, shurikin, or stun gun outside the person's own home.

Type of Crime: Class 2 Misdemeanor

Punishment: Community punishment with up to 30 days in jail for failure to comply

VII. Property: Your Property and the Property of Others

Chapter 23
Stealing

Shoplifting

Two women entered an upscale department store in a mall. They both were carrying bags containing purchases from other stores. They believed no one was watching them, and they placed several expensive items in their bags and exited the store without paying for the merchandise. They were immediately apprehended by store security and arrested for shoplifting. Their theft was recorded on high-definition digital recording. The recording was so clear you could read the numbers on the price tags! Both women were charged with the felony crime of shoplifting.

Most establishments today have high-tech surveillance equipment that allows store personnel to observe and record a shopper's every move. Just because you do not see anyone does not mean someone is not watching.

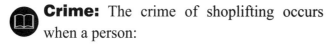 **Crime:** The crime of shoplifting occurs when a person:

- Takes property that has a value of more than $200, by using an exit door that bears notice regarding the felony offense and the relevant punishment, to exit the store;

- Removes, destroys, or deactivates a component of an anti-shoplifting or inventory control device to prevent activation of any anti-shoplifting or inventory control device;

- Affixes a product code created for the purpose of fraudulently obtaining goods or merchandise from a merchant at less than its actual price; OR

- Takes infant formula valued in excess of $100.

Type of Crime: Class H Felony

Punishment: Community, intermediate, or active punishment with a minimum of 5 months imprisonment for active punishment or failure to comply with community or intermediate punishment

If a person takes property from a merchant that is valued at $200 or less, then the crime is a Class 1 Misdemeanor, punishable by community punishment with up to 45 days in jail for failure to comply.

> **Example:** *P places a jacket worth $175 in an empty shopping bag and leaves the store with it without paying for it. P is guilty of misdemeanor shoplifting because the retail value of the item is less than $200. If the jacket was worth $275, P would be guilty of a felony.*

Concealment of Merchandise in Stores

Crime: The crime of concealment of merchandise occurs when a person in a commercial establishment willfully conceals store merchandise not purchased while still on the premises.

> **Example:** *P is in a clothing store with a shopping bag from another store. P places three tops in the shopping bag. P is guilty of concealment of merchandise in stores.*

Additionally, a person is guilty of concealment of merchandise in commercial establishments when the person transfers any price tag from goods to other goods having a higher selling price or marks goods at a lower price and then presents the goods for purchase.

> **Example:** *P changes the price tag on a jacket from $150 to $50, goes to the cash register, and pays $50 for the jacket. P is guilty of concealment of merchandise in stores, which is a misdemeanor.*

Type of Crime: Class 3 Misdemeanor

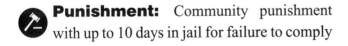 **Punishment:** Community punishment with up to 10 days in jail for failure to comply

Pay Attention!
The storekeeper can also sue you civilly for two times the full retail value of the shoplifted items.

Theft

Crime: The crime of theft (larceny) occurs when a person takes and carries away the personal property of another person without consent with the intent to deny the true owner the use of the property permanently.

If the property is worth over $1,000 (or in the case of shoplifting, is worth over $200), a felony has been committed. If the property is worth $1,000 or less (or in the case of shoplifting, is worth $200 or less), a misdemeanor has been committed.

Type of Crime: Over $1,000 (or over $200 in case of shoplifting) – Class H Felony; $1,000 or less (or $200 or less in case of shoplifting) – Class 1 Misdemeanor

Punishment: Class H Felony – Community, intermediate, or active punishment with a minimum of 5 months imprisonment for active punishment or for failure to comply with community or intermediate punishment; Class 1 Misdemeanor – Community punishment with up to 45 days in jail for failure to comply

Example: *P takes a laptop from the library with intent to steal. P is guilty of felony larceny if the laptop is worth more than $1,000.*

Theft by Receiving Stolen Property

College students can get in serious trouble for being in possession of something that was stolen, such as an iPod, laptop, or stereo system. This is where common sense should take control. If the deal you are getting is "too good to be true," it probably is *not* true. Do not buy *anything* unless you know who the true owner is. This warning also applies if you borrow something that is stolen, such as a car. If you are not absolutely sure that the rightful owner of a vehicle has given you permission to drive the car, don't get behind the wheel.

❓ Did You Know that theft by receiving stolen property and shoplifting are crimes of equal weight and punishment?

Example: *P purchases a brand-new, in-the-box MacBook® from a friend for $200. P should know that the laptop was probably not obtained legally. Nevertheless, P keeps and uses the laptop. P can be charged with theft by receiving stolen property.*

📖 **Crime:** The crime of theft by receiving stolen property occurs when a person receives, disposes, retains, or keeps stolen property that the person knows is stolen property or had reasonable grounds to believe is stolen property.

Type of Crime: Possession of stolen property worth more than $1,000 – Class H Felony; possession of stolen property worth $1,000 or less – Class 1 Misdemeanor

Punishment: Class H Felony – Community, intermediate, or active punishment with a minimum of 5 months imprisonment for active punishment or for failure to comply with community or intermediate punishment; Class 1 Misdemeanor – Community punishment with up to 45 days in jail for failure to comply

Stealing From Your Employer

Did You Know that it is a felony to steal from your employer, regardless of the value of what is stolen?

Crime: The crime of larceny by employee is committed when an employee takes from an employer with the intent to steal or defraud the employer.

Type of Crime: Any amount under $100,000, no matter how little, is a Class H Felony

Punishment: Community, intermediate, or active punishment with a minimum of 5 months imprisonment for active punishment or for failure to comply with community or intermediate punishment

Example: *P works at a local bar as a bartender. P serves food and drinks valued at $150 to P's friends and does not charge them. P is guilty of a Class H Felony, and P's friends are guilty of theft by receiving stolen property, a Class 1 Misdemeanor for items valued under $200.*

Example: *P1 works at a clothing store. P1's friend, P2, comes to the store to buy a coat. When P2 brings a coat worth $100 to the cash register, P1 types in a code instead of scanning the merchandise and only charges P2 $10. P1 is guilty of a Class H Felony, and P2 is guilty of theft, a Class 1 Misdemeanor.*

Chapter 24
Invading Another Person's Property

Trespass

Crime: Trespass in the first-degree occurs when a person enters another's premises that are enclosed or secured so as to demonstrate a clear intent to keep out intruders, or enters another's building without permission.

Type of Crime: Class 2 Misdemeanor

Punishment: Community punishment with up to 30 days in jail

> **Example:** *P leaves P's jacket and wallet in a fraternity house during a party. The next morning, P returns to the house to retrieve P's belongings, but the house is locked and the guys are still asleep inside. P climbs in through a window of the fraternity house to get P's jacket and wallet. P is guilty of first-degree trespass.*

Crime: Trespass in the second-degree occurs when a person without authorization enters or remains on another's premises 1) despite notice by the other person not to enter or remain on the premises or 2) despite a reasonable posting not to enter the premises.

Type of Crime: Class 3 Misdemeanor

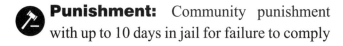 **Punishment:** Community punishment with up to 10 days in jail for failure to comply

Example: *A "No Trespassing" sign is posted on V's property in several visible locations. P uses V's property as a shortcut between the campus parking lot and P's dorm. P is guilty of second-degree trespass.*

Injury to Real and Personal Property

Students from a first-year hall decide to play a prank on the sophomores upstairs. They throw eggs at their dorm room windows and clog the toilets in the hall bathroom. The first-year students are guilty of willful and wanton injury to real property.

Did You Know that rolling a house in toilet paper or throwing eggs at a person's house is a crime?

Crime: The crime of willful and wanton injury to real or personal property occurs when a person willfully and wantonly destroys or injures any real or personal property, private or public.

Real property refers to land, buildings, and fixtures to land or buildings; personal property refers to moveable items, such as furniture, computers, cars, and clothes.

Type of Crime: All real property damages and all personal property damages over $200 – Class

1 Misdemeanor; personal property damages $200 and less – Class 2 Misdemeanor

Punishment: Class 1 Misdemeanor – community punishment with up to 45 days in jail for failure to comply; Class 2 Misdemeanor – community punishment with up to 30 days in jail for failure to comply

> **Example:** *P returns to P's apartment late at night after a party. P is drunk and starts throwing the flower pots owned by the apartment complex around the parking lot and through windows in the clubhouse. P is guilty of willful and wanton injury to personal property for breaking the flower pots; P is guilty of willful and wanton injury to real property for any damage to the clubhouse.*

Burglary

Crime: The crime of burglary occurs when a person breaks and enters a dwelling house or sleeping apartment of another in the nighttime (after dark) with the intent to commit a felony or larceny.

The crime of burglary has two degrees. *First-degree burglary* is committed when the house or apartment is occupied at the time of the breaking and entering. *Second-degree burglary* is committed when the house or apartment is unoccupied at the time of the breaking and entering.

"Dwelling house" or "sleeping apartment" includes almost any structure in which a person would or does sleep.

Type of Crime: First-Degree Burglary – Class D Felony; Second-Degree Burglary – Class G Felony

Punishment: Class D Felony – active punishment with a minimum of 51 months imprisonment; Class G Felony – intermediate or active punishment with a minimum of 10 months imprisonment for active punishment or for failure to comply with intermediate punishment

Example: *P breaks into V's apartment at nighttime with intent to steal a laptop, thinking the apartment is unoccupied because V is on vacation. However, V's friend is crashing there while V is away, and V's friend is in the apartment asleep. Because the apartment is occupied, P is guilty of first-degree burglary.*

If you do not intend to steal something or commit a felony, you are guilty of a Class 1 Misdemeanor.

Pay Attention!
If you commit burglary with the intent to steal something, you commit a felony regardless of the value of the item.

Breaking and Entering

Crime: The crime of breaking and entering occurs when any person breaks and enters into any building with the intent to commit a felony or larceny.

Type of Crime: Class H Felony

Punishment: Community, intermediate, or active punishment with a minimum of 5 months imprisonment for active punishment or for failure to comply with community or intermediate punishment

If you do not intend to steal something or commit a felony, you are guilty of a Class 1 Misdemeanor.

Pay Attention!
This crime includes breaking into a shed, barn, or garage.

Pay Attention!
If you commit breaking and entering with the intent to steal something, you commit a felony regardless of the value of the item.

Breaking and Entering a Building That is a Place of Religious Worship

Crime: The crime of breaking and entering a building that is a place of religious worship occurs when a person wrongly breaks and enters into a building that is a place of religious worship with the intent to commit any felony or larceny.

Type of crime: Class G Felony

Punishment: Intermediate or active punishment with a minimum of 10 months imprisonment for active punishment or for failure to comply with intermediate punishment

If you do not intend to steal something or commit a felony, you are guilty of a Class 1 Misdemeanor.

Breaking and Entering into a Motor Vehicle

Crime: The crime of breaking and entering into a motor vehicle occurs when a person breaks and enters into a motor vehicle, boat, watercraft, trailer, or railway car.

Type of Crime: Class I Felony

Punishment: Community punishment with a minimum of 4 months imprisonment for failure to comply

Chapter 25
Intellectual Property and Electronic Crimes

Piracy

Crime: The crime of piracy occurs when a person makes unauthorized copies of copyrighted material.

Type of Crime and Punishment: The type of crime and the type of punishment are governed by federal law and depend on the circumstances.

This crime includes downloading music or movies from peer-to-peer sites, where you do not pay for the contents you are obtaining, and copying a friend's CD or DVD onto your computer or another CD/DVD for your use. If you aren't sure if what you are doing is legal, you can refer to www.riaa.com for more information on piracy and the law.

Computer Trespass

Crime: The crime of computer trespass occurs when a person goes on a computer server and deletes or alters the personal data information of another person without that person's permission.

Type of Crime: Class 3 Misdemeanor

Punishment: Community punishment with up to 10 days in jail for failure to comply

Example: *P and V are in a romantic relationship, and even more, they are in a Facebook® relationship. V breaks up with P, who is now upset and semi-heartbroken. While they were on happier terms, P learned V's Facebook® password. P logs onto V's Facebook® account and changes V's personal information, including V's relationship status, "Looking For," and "About Me" sections, without V's knowledge. P is guilty of a Class 3 Misdemeanor.*

Exception: If computer trespass causes damage to another person's property valued at less than $2500, the crime is a Class 1 Misdemeanor. If the damage is $2500 or more, then the crime is a Class I Felony.

Sharing your passwords or allowing another person to use your account may be a violation of your school's computer system Terms of Use Policy or Honor Code. Read your Student Handbook.

Pay Attention!
Do not share your computer passwords with another person or use another person's passwords! In addition, if you find out that another person has your password, change it. Be in the regular practice of frequently changing your passwords.

Other Electronic Crimes

Other crimes involving electronic equipment discussed in this book include the following:

- **Sexting and sexual exploitation of a minor, first-degree, second-degree, and third-degree** – *See Chapter Sixteen, Sexting and Sexual Exploitation of Minors*

- **Solicitation of a child (under 16 years old) by computer to commit an unlawful sex act** – *See Chapter Twenty-Nine, More Crimes Against Children and Reporting Child Abuse*

- **Cyberstalking** – *See Chapter Nineteen, Safety and Bodily Harm*

> **Example:** *Using a file-sharing site, **P** downloads pornography labeled "attractive twentysomethings." However, the file actually depicts adolescents. **P**, realizing after the download that the file is not what **P** was looking for, places the file in the Recycle Bin – but does not adequately and permanently delete it from the computer. **P** is now guilty of third-degree sexual exploitation of a minor, a felony, for possessing sexually explicit material featuring minors.*

Downloading illegal copies of music, videos, or software may also violate your school's Terms of Usage Policy or Honor Code. Downloading even legal (non-obscene) pornography may also violate your school's computer system Terms of Use Policy or Honor Code. Read your Student Handbook.

VIII. Staying the Course: Driving, Driving Violations, and Accidents

Chapter 26
What to Do if You Are Pulled Over or in an Accident

Chapter 27
Other Driving Violations

Chapter 26
What to Do if You Are Pulled Over or in an Accident

If You Are Pulled Over

Here are suggested procedures if you are stopped in your vehicle by the police.

What to Do:

- Pull off the road on the right side of the highway, or, if there are more than two lanes in the same direction, pull off on the safest side.

- Remain seated in your vehicle, put your vehicle in the parked position, and turn on your emergency flashers and your interior lights (if you are stopped at night).

- Turn off your radio or music, put both hands on the steering wheel, and ask passengers to put hands in their laps.

- Lower your window to talk to the officer.

What Not to Do:

- Do not talk or send messages on your cell phone.

- Do not move around your vehicle (*e.g.*, do not reach under the seats or open the glove box or center console).

- Do not get out of your vehicle or allow your

passengers to get out of your vehicle, unless requested by the officer.

Make sure you have your driver's license, the registration of the vehicle, and proof of insurance, especially if it's not your car (*e.g.*, you're the designated driver in your friend's car). Also, if you have a fake ID, do *not* hand it to the police when you're pulled over. This happens way too often, both by accident (drivers get nervous and give the first thing they find in their wallets) and when people under 21 think they won't get in trouble if the cops think they're of legal age. As pointed out in Chapter Ten, you will be in a *lot* more trouble if you give a police officer a fake ID instead of your own, even if you have alcohol in the vehicle.

Be polite to the police, and say "Yes, Sir," or "No, Ma'am." Do not lie to the cops, but do not talk yourself into trouble, either. If you are asked any incriminating questions, request to call your attorney before you say anything else.

Trying to talk your way out of an arrest will probably just lead to more trouble. People rarely talk their way out of trouble, but many talk their way into trouble. Remember, fish get caught for two reasons: 1) they open their mouths, or 2) they are swimming with the wrong school of fish and got caught in the net. Be careful what you say and whom you are around.

Searching your vehicle

If you are stopped, make sure you haven't given

the officer probable cause to search your car. A cloud of marijuana smoke in the vehicle would be a reason for searching the car. Also, a visible open container of alcohol in the car will result in a search. If the officer can see anything that looks suspicious – a beer bottle on the floor, small plastic bags with something green in them, a weapon – through any of the car windows, the officer likely has probable cause to search your car.

If you are stopped for a traffic violation, an officer may ask permission to search your car. Remember, you do not have to give consent to search your car, no matter how much pressure the officer puts on you. If you give consent, even if the officer had no probable cause to search your car, you have waived your rights. Also, the fact that you did not give consent cannot be used as a basis for the officers to search the vehicle.

Officers will try to pressure you into giving consent by saying, "I can get a search warrant if you don't give me consent to search your car, so why don't you make it easy on both of us and just consent to a search." If you refuse to give consent, politely tell the officer you are not giving consent to search your vehicle.

Remember, if the officer actually has probable cause to search a car, the officer doesn't have to get a search warrant or ask for permission to search your car.

Some officers will try to entice a student, even

lie to a student, to get consent to search the car. Threatening to get a search warrant is a way for the officer to try to get you to give consent. You do *not* have to consent.

The officer may separate the driver from the passengers. The officer may then tell the driver that the passengers told the officer contraband is in the car. Whether the passengers have said anything at all is irrelevant; the driver may now think that giving consent to a search is necessary – even though legally the driver does *not* have to consent. Unfortunately, there is no prohibition against the police tricking someone into giving consent.

Who gets arrested if illegal things (alcohol, drugs, etc.) are in the car?

If contraband is found in the cab of the vehicle, the driver and the passengers will be arrested. Any person who has access to the contraband will be presumed to be in possession. If the contraband is found only on one person (*e.g.*, inside a pocket, or inside the person's purse or wallet), there's a chance only that person will be arrested. However, you all could be arrested, and the lawyers needed to fight possession charges are very expensive.

If you are under 21 years old and have been drinking, you will be considered to have broken the law, no matter how much or how little alcohol is on your breath. The only question is whether you are guilty of **Driving After Consuming Alcohol or Drugs** or the more serious **Driving While Impaired**. *See Chapter Fourteen, Drinking, Drugs, and Driving.*

If You Are in a Car Accident

If you are in an accident on a public highway or street, you must stop at the scene of the accident and call the police and report the accident. If the accident occurs on private property, such as a driveway or parking lot, and no one is injured, you must still stop at the scene of the accident, but you do not have to notify the police.

You need to exchange names, addresses, phone numbers, driver's license number, license plate number, make and model of car, and insurance information with the other driver any time you are involved in an accident.

Chapter 27
Other Driving Violations

Death by Vehicle

Felony Crime: The crime of felony death by vehicle occurs when a person, without planning or intent, causes the death of another while driving under the influence of alcohol or drugs.

Type of Crime: Class E Felony

Punishment: Intermediate or active punishment with a minimum of 20 months imprisonment for active punishment or for failure to comply with intermediate punishment

> **Example:** *P is driving home from a party in the woods where P and P's friends had a few beers around the campfire. P hits V, who is out walking V's dog at night. V dies. P is guilty of felony death by vehicle.*

Misdemeanor Crime: The crime of misdemeanor death by vehicle occurs when a person, without planning or intent, causes the death of another while engaged in a violation of any State law or local ordinance applying to the operation or use of a vehicle or to a traffic regulation.

Type of Crime: Class 1 Misdemeanor

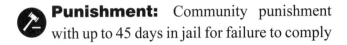 **Punishment:** Community punishment with up to 45 days in jail for failure to comply

> **Example:** *P hits and kills a pedestrian while making an illegal left turn. P is guilty of misdemeanor death by vehicle.*

Reckless Driving

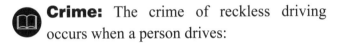 **Crime:** The crime of reckless driving occurs when a person drives:

- Carelessly or in willful or wanton disregard of the rights or safety of others; OR

- Without due caution and care and at a speed or in a manner so as to endanger or likely endanger any person or property.

Type of Crime: Class 2 Misdemeanor

Punishment: Community punishment with up to 30 days in jail for failure to comply

> **Example:** *P is arrested for driving P's car at a high rate of speed at night without lights on. P is guilty of reckless driving.*

Racing on Highways and Streets

Crime: The crime of racing on highways and streets occurs when a person does any of the following:

- Participates willfully in a pre-arranged speed competition on a highway or street with another vehicle;

- Participates willfully in a speed competition on a highway or street with another vehicle;

- Authorizes or permits a motor vehicle owned by the person or under the person's control to be operated on a street or highway in a pre-arranged speed competition with another vehicle; OR

- Places or receives any bet, wager, or other thing of value from the outcome of any pre-arranged speed competition on a street or highway.

Type of Crime: First, third, and fourth bullet points – Class 1 Misdemeanor; second bullet point – Class 2 Misdemeanor

Punishment: Class 1 Misdemeanor – Community punishment with up to 45 days in jail for failure to comply; Class 2 Misdemeanor – Community punishment with up to 30 days in jail; and, for all convictions, up to 3-year revocation of your driver's license. The car can also be taken from you and sold by the state.

Aggressive Driving

Crime: The crime of aggressive driving occurs when a person 1) operates a motor vehicle on a street, highway, or public vehicular area in violation of speed limits or school speed zone limits, and 2) drives carelessly in willful or wanton disregard of the rights or safety of others. Driving carelessly occurs if a driver commits any TWO OR MORE of the following:

• Running through a red light;

• Running through a stop sign;

• Illegally passing;

• Failing to yield right-of-way; OR

• Following too closely.

Type of Crime: Class 1 Misdemeanor

 Punishment: Community punishment with up to 45 days in jail for failure to comply

Hit-and-Run; Leaving the Scene of an Accident

A college student was on the way home from a recreational soccer game when a child riding a bike darted out in front of the car and was struck and killed. The accident was unavoidable, and the driver of the car was in no way at fault. Unfortunately, in a state of panic, the driver fled the scene and went straight back to her apartment to call her parents instead of waiting for the police. Had she stayed at the scene of the accident, she would not have faced any charges. Because she left the scene, she was charged with felony hit-and-run.

? Did You Know that you commit a crime if you leave the scene of a car accident?

Crime: The crime of hit-and-run or leaving the scene of an accident occurs when a person involved in an accident resulting in injury to a person or damage to a vehicle fails to stop at the scene of the accident (or as close as possible to the accident) and fails to provide the following:

- Name, address, license plate number, and driver's license number; AND

- Reasonable assistance to any injured person, including making arrangements for transporting a person to receive medical treatment.

Leaving the scene of an accident only adds more problems. And if you stay, you may find out that you were not even at fault for the cause of the accident.

Type of Crime: Felony if the accident is the proximate cause of death or a serious injury; misdemeanor if the accident is the proximate cause of damage to vehicle or non-serious injury to person.

Punishment: Felony – up to 16 months imprisonment; Misdemeanor – up to 45 days imprisonment *and* 1-year revocation of your driver's license

Striking an Unattended Vehicle

Have you ever parked your car in a parking lot and returned to find that someone had crunched your bumper or a door panel and did not leave you a note? If so, whoever hit your car just committed a crime.

Crime: A crime occurs when a person fails to notify the owner or operator of an unattended vehicle that the person strikes.

Type of Crime: Class 3 Misdemeanor

Punishment: Community punishment with up to 10 days in jail for failure to comply

Pay Attention!
If you strike an unattended vehicle, try to locate the vehicle's operator or owner and notify that person of both your name and address and the name and address of your vehicle's owner. Or, leave a note in an obvious place on the vehicle with your name and address and the name and address of your vehicle's owner.

Allowing a Person to Drive without a License

Crime: A crime occurs when a person knowingly permits any unlicensed minor under the age of 18 years old to drive a motor vehicle on any highway.

Type of Crime: Class 2 Misdemeanor

Punishment: Community punishment with up to 30 days in jail for failure to comply

Did You Know
that you commit a crime if you strike a parked vehicle and fail to find the owner or leave a note?

Did You Know
that you commit a crime if you let an unlicensed person under 18 drive your car?

Unlawful Driving of a Pick-Up Truck

 **Crime:** A crime occurs when the driver of a pick-up truck allows a person under 16 years old to ride in the bed of the pick-up truck.

Exceptions:

- An adult is present in the bed and supervising the child;

- The child is secured by a seat belt manufactured with the vehicle;

- There is an emergency situation;

- The vehicle is in a parade; OR

- The vehicle is being operated by an agricultural enterprise.

Punishment: Fine

Points for Speeding and Other Driving Violations

If you are guilty of a driving violation, you will receive driving points on your personal motor vehicle record, with more serious violations receiving higher points. Driving points can increase the cost of your insurance, result in the suspension of your driver's license, and delay your ability to apply for your subsequent license.

In North Carolina, if you accumulate 12 points

Driving Violation Points

Violation	Points
Passing stopped school bus	5
Aggressive driving	5
Reckless driving	4
Hit and run, property damage only	4
Following too closely	4
Illegal passing	4
Failure to yield right-of-way to pedestrian	4
Running through stop sign	3
Running through red light	3
Speeding in a school zone in excess of the posted school zone speed limit	3
Littering, when the littering involves the use of a motor vehicle	1

within a 3-year period, your license may be suspended.

The chart on the previous page is a partial list of the assignment of points for certain driving violations.

❗ Pay Attention!
Driving more than 15 miles per hour over the posted speed limit can result in the revocation of your driver's license for 30 days.

The loss of your license due to the "15 miles per hour" rule applies whenever you are driving at a speed higher than 55 miles per hour (*e.g.*, if you are pulled over for driving 61 miles per hour in a 45 miles per hour zone or 71 miles per hour in a 55 miles per hour zone).

❗ Pay Attention!
Driving over 80 miles per hour – no matter the speed limit of the road on which you are traveling – will result in the revocation of your driver's license for at least 30 days.

❗ Pay Attention!
If you see an emergency vehicle pulled off to the right-hand side of the road, you are required by law, if possible to do so safely, to move over to the left-hand lane while passing the vehicle.

❗ Pay Attention!
If you are convicted of a driving offense in another state that results in a loss of your license in that state, it will also result in the loss of your license

in your home state. Also, if you are convicted of a driving offense in another state that would result in loss of your license in your home state but not in the other state, your home state can revoke your license based on an out-of-state conviction.

❶ Pay Attention!

North Carolina prohibits the use of additional technology (such as text messaging or e-mail) on a mobile phone while driving. Punishment is a $100 fine and court costs.

IX. Other Criminal Laws and Topics of Interest: Groups and Group Initiations, Crimes Against Children, and More

Chapter 28
Common Crimes Committed by Groups or During Group Initiations

This chapter discusses both the crime of hazing and crimes commonly committed in group situations or during group initiation activities. Many of the crimes in this chapter may be found elsewhere in this book; the related examples here, though, reflect frequent or real situations that have occurred on college campuses.

In most cases, individuals may not think they are committing a crime or may not intend to commit a crime. Sometimes activities get out of control, or alcohol interferes with judgment, and crimes result. As noted earlier in the book, with most crimes, your intent to commit a *crime* is not important. What is important is your intent to commit the *act* that results in the crime.

Many acts of membership initiation could be classified either as hazing, criminal acts, or both. In some situations, the people and group conducting the activities could be guilty of multiple crimes (including, but not limited to, hazing).

Hazing

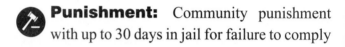 **Crime:** The crime of hazing is committed when any student of a university, college, or school subjects another student to physical injury as part of an initiation or prerequisite to membership into any organized school group, including any society, athletic team, fraternity or sorority, or other similar group.

Type of Crime: Class 2 Misdemeanor

Punishment: Community punishment with up to 30 days in jail for failure to comply

> **Example:** *As part of pledging, one activity involves drinking beer every time a song changes over the course of an hour ("Power Hour"). At the end of the hour, one of the pledges becomes ill with alcohol poisoning and is taken to the emergency room. The fraternity leaders may be charged with hazing.*

Alcohol, Drugs, and Parties

Purchase, Possession, or Consumption of Alcohol by Persons Under 21 Years Old

P is under the age of 21 and consumes beer at a frat party. On the way back to the dorm, a police officer stops P and asks for P's name. The officer smells alcohol on P's breath, and arrests P for underage consumption of alcohol (beer), a Class 3 Misdemeanor. P tells the officer the name of *the fraternity. After placing **P** in handcuffs, the officer drives over to the fraternity to arrest the people who provided the alcohol to **P** and charges them with furnishing alcohol to minors, a Class 1 Misdemeanor. Both **P** and the alcohol providers will have their driver's licenses revoked for one year.* **See Chapter Nine, Alcohol and Underage Drinking.**

Furnishing Alcohol to Minors

A few seniors on the soccer team, all 21 years old or older, host an Around-the-World for first-year students joining the men and women's soccer teams. The first-year students travel from apartment to apartment, drinking a different soccer-themed drink at each apartment. The seniors, who purchased the liquor for the drinks, are committing the crime of furnishing alcohol to minors, a Class 1 Misdemeanor. The seniors will have a separate charge for each attendee under the age of 21. The seniors can also be charged with aiding and abetting underage consumption and underage possession. The first-year students will be charged with underage consumption and underage possession of alcohol (liquor), both Class 1 Misdemeanors (unless a first-year student is 19 or 20, in which case consumption will be a Class 3 Misdemeanor). Both the seniors and the first-year students will have their driver's licenses revoked for a year. **See Chapter Nine, Alcohol and Underage Drinking.**

The men's and women's track teams host a party after the season ends. The first-year runners are *assigned the task of setting up the party on a Friday afternoon after class. A senior purchases the alcohol for the party and then gives the first-year runners instructions to move the alcohol from the senior's car into the apartment where the party will be held. A police officer notices the senior's car in the fire lane as the first-year runners are unloading the cases and handles of liquor into the apartment. The officer arrests each of the under-21-year-old runners for possession of alcohol by a minor, a Class 1 Misdemeanor (unless the runners are 19 or 20, in which case possession of beer is a Class 3 Misdemeanor). The officer then gets a warrant to arrest the senior who purchased the alcohol and charges the senior with one count of furnishing alcohol to minors for each under-21-year-old student the officer arrested, a Class 1 Misdemeanor, along with aiding and abetting underage possession of alcohol. In addition, the driver's licenses of the first-year students and the senior will be revoked for a year. **See Chapter Nine, Alcohol and Underage Drinking.***

Driving After Consuming Alcohol or Drugs (Under 21 Years Old)

A 19-year-old pledge received a text to report immediately to an off-campus house belonging to a member of the sorority. The pledge, who at the time was watching a rom-com movie in the dorm with her roommate, is not drunk; however, she has had a couple of mixed drinks during the movie. The pledge hops into her car and drives to the off-campus house; along the way, a police officer pulls her over for a burned-out taillight. Even though

*she passes the field sobriety test, she registers 0.05
on the breathalyzer test. The pledge is arrested for
driving after consuming alcohol or drugs, a Class
2 Misdemeanor, and will have her driver's license
revoked for 1 year.* **See Chapter Nine, Alcohol and
Underage Drinking.**

Drunk and Disorderly Conduct; Public Urination

*A fraternity has a party at a hotel on the beach.
Two members of the fraternity, who are drunk, start
scuffling with each other during a beach volleyball
game. The two members may be arrested for drunk
and disorderly conduct. At the same party, several
members of the fraternity decide to pee off the
hotel balcony instead of waiting in line for the
bathroom. These members may be charged with
public urination. Again, at the same party, other
members of the fraternity pull the fire alarm at the
hotel at 3:00 a.m. as a prank. These members may
be charged with pulling a false fire alarm, a Class
2 Misdemeanor.* **See Chapter Nine, Alcohol and
Underage Drinking and Chapter Thirty, Other
Laws of Interest.**

Using, Making, Selling, or Distributing False Identification

*Upon initiation to the sorority, each of the Big
Sisters for the new initiates orders a new driver's
license from her state's DMV. The Big Sisters give*

their old licenses to the Littles who resemble them. The Big Sisters are guilty of a Class 1 Misdemeanor if their Little Sisters intend to purchase alcohol or obtain anything of value. If the Little Sisters use the IDs of other people to try to purchase alcohol or obtain anything of value (such as admission to a bar), the Little Sisters are committing a Class G Felony for using the ID of another (real) person. If caught and convicted, both the Big Sisters and the Little Sisters will have their driver's licenses revoked for 1 year. **See Chapter Ten, Fake IDs and Misrepresentation of Age.**

The news editor of the school newspaper makes fake driver's licenses using the printing equipment for the newspaper and provides the fake IDs to the underage reporters before the staff retreat. The editor is committing a Class I Felony for making and distributing fake IDs that simulated driver's licenses. If the reporters use the fake IDs to try to purchase alcohol or obtain anything of value (such as admission to a bar), they are committing a Class 1 Misdemeanor and will have their driver's licenses revoked for 1 year. **See Chapter Ten, Fake IDs and Misrepresentation of Age.**

Social Host Liability

After an off-campus pledge activity, where older members have provided alcohol to the pledges during a double elimination beer pong tournament, one of the pledges gets in a car and drives back to the dorm. Along the way, the pledge runs a red light and hits another car, causing serious damage to the car and injuring its driver. The hosts of the beer pong tourney could be found liable for the injuries and damages caused by the pledge's accident. **See Chapter Nine, Alcohol and Underage Drinking.**

Trafficking in Cocaine

Initiation for a fraternity is scheduled to take place at a farm off-campus. Six of the brothers decide to pool their money to purchase an ounce of cocaine to split among them. One of the brothers in the group purchases the cocaine and carpools with three other brothers in the group to the farm. On the way, the police stop them, and the cocaine is discovered. Every person in the car is considered to be trafficking in cocaine and is committing a Class G Felony, a crime with a minimum punishment of 35 months in prison. The two brothers in the group who contributed money to the purchase of the cocaine but who are not in the car are guilty as accessories before the fact and will receive the same punishment as those in the car. **See Chapter Eleven, Possession and Sale of Legal and Illegal Drugs, and Chapter Four, Parties to a Crime.**

Property Crimes

Criminal Trespass

A large pond is located in a neighborhood where many students rent houses. The pond is on private property (i.e., is not a public part of the neighborhood). There is no house on the property.

In the past, students were allowed to swim in the pond and sunbathe on the dock. When the property is sold to new owners, the new owners post "No Trespassing" signs. The students continue to swim in the pond. The students are arrested for second-degree trespass, a Class 3 Misdemeanor. **See Chapter Twenty-Four, Invading Another Person's Property.**

Breaking and Entering

The first-year students on the football team are assigned the prank of breaking into the basketball team's locker room to steal the players' jerseys. Because the first-year football players break into the locker room to commit larceny, they are guilty of the crime of breaking and entering, a Class H Felony, regardless of whether they take the jerseys. **See Chapter Twenty-Four, Invading Another Person's Property.**

Theft

A fraternity throws a large party at its house after a football game. A few of a brother's friends drop by the party on the way home from the game. After raiding the stash of brownies, having a few drinks from the alcohol cabinet, and playing a few video games, the mooching visitors find the fraternity's historic crest in one of the rooms. The visitors realize that sneaking the large, pool table-sized crest out of this house and through the raging party is a near-impossible feat; of course, they then plot to accomplish the task. Somehow, mission impossible succeeds as the visitors manage to sneak a 200-pound giant shield out of a party with

100 people. The thieves get home. They celebrate. They give the crest to their roommates as a present. A couple of months later, after the shield has been used and abused as a beer pong table and decorative lawn art, police officers arrive with a warrant to arrest the thieves for theft of an item worth over $1,000, a Class H Felony. (Apparently the shield was custom-made.) The roommates, who were given the crest as a gift, are arrested for theft by receiving stolen property worth over $1,000, a Class H Felony. **See Chapter Twenty-Three, Stealing.**

Burglary

Two fraternity pledges are told to break into the neighboring sorority house and steal a pair of panties from each of the bedrooms. The pledges decide to do this over a long holiday weekend, when the house is likely to be vacant. The pledges break in at midnight, and after a couple of successful panty swipes, the pledges enter the third bedroom, only to find a girl sleeping inside. The pledges are guilty of first-degree burglary, a Class D Felony, regardless of the value of the panties they are stealing. **See Chapter Twenty-Four, Invading Another Person's Property.**

Injury to Property

The pledge activity of the night is to give a neighboring rival house a facelift and take pictures to upload to Facebook®. The pledges cut bushes into phallic shapes, spray paint the front door, and color the grass with weed killer. The pledges are committing the crime of injury to real and personal *property, a Class 1 Misdemeanor. **See Chapter Twenty-Four, Invading Another's Person's Property.***

Gambling

*Organization **P** sponsors an annual March Madness pool, with a $20 buy-in per person. The organizers and participants are committing the crime of gambling, a Class 2 Misdemeanor. **See Chapter Thirty, Other Laws of Interest.***

Possession of a Weapon on Campus or Other Educational Property

*Campus police officers notice the local college Ultimate Frisbee team playing a midnight game on the quad. When the officers walk up to the students, the officers notice cases of beer on the sidelines and smell marijuana smoke. When the officers search the students, who smell like the lawn of Bonnaroo, they do not find marijuana; however, one of the officers discovers a switchblade knife in a student's pocket. The student is arrested for misdemeanor possession of a weapon on campus, a Class 1 Misdemeanor. **See Chapter Twenty-Two, Weapons and Firearms.***

Harm to People
Sexual Offense
V has too much to drink at a frat party and passes

out on the basement couch. One of the party's attendees, **P1***, dares another person,* **P2***, to "teabag"* **V** *while* **P1** *photographs the moment.* **P2** *is committing the crime of second-degree sexual offense, a Class C Felony;* **P1** *is committing the crime of aiding and abetting and will be charged with the same offense as* **P2***.* **See Chapter Fifteen, Sex Crimes with Force and Chapter Four, Parties to a Crime.**

Sexual Battery

V has too much to drink at a frat party and passes out on the basement couch. One of the party's attendees, **P1***, persuades* **P2** *to straddle V and masturbate while* **P1** *videos the moment.* **P2** *is committing the crime of sexual battery, a Class A1 Misdemeanor;* **P1** *is committing the crime of aiding and abetting and will be charged with the same offense as* **P2***.* **See Chapter Fifteen, Sex Crimes with Force, and Chapter Four, Parties to a Crime.**

Rape

P *and* **V** *attend a Greek-sponsored handcuff party, where* **P** *and* **V** *are bound together until they finish a fifth of liquor. While handcuffed,* **V** *shows an interest in* **P***: she flirts, she caresses, and she makes flattering comments about* **P's** *buff biceps.* **V***, a small female, quickly becomes intoxicated.* **P***, who has been attached to* **V** *and watched her drink, knows this, and knows that* **V** *has probably blacked out given the amount of alcohol* **V** *consumed in an hour.* **P** *and* **V** *begin hooking up, and they end up having sex. Under the law,* **P** *committed second-degree rape, a Class C Felony with a minimum of*

58 months imprisonment. **See Chapter Fifteen, Sex Crimes with Force.**

P1 laces V's drink with roofies at a fraternity party. P1 and P2 then take V to an upstairs bedroom. While V is incapacitated, P1 and P2 proceed to have sex with V. P1 and P2 will both be charged with second-degree rape, a Class C Felony, and P1 will be charged with putting roofies in V's drink, a Class G Felony. If P2 encouraged P1 to put roofies in V's drink, P2 committed the crime of aiding and abetting and will also be charged with a Class G Felony. **See Chapter Fifteen, Sex Crimes with Force.**

Assault

A fraternity hosts a closed party. An uninvited guest, P1, tries to enter, threatening the doorman – a pledge – and attempting to push his way inside. The doorman calls out to a brother, P2, who proceeds to get in a brawl with the party crasher. P1 ends up with a black eye after receiving a few punches; P2 ends up with a concussion after falling to the ground. Both P1 and P2 committed assault and battery that resulted in serious injury to another person, a Class A1 Misdemeanor. **See Chapter Nineteen, Threats to Safety and Bodily Harm.**

Felonious Restraint

Brand new pledges are told to report to the house at 9 p.m. on a Friday night. The pledges are divided into groups, blindfolded, and placed into cars driven by older students. Once in the cars, the pledges are told they are heading on a scavenger hunt. One of the pledges tells the driver that the pledge no longer wants to be a part of this activity and asks to return back to the house. The pledge says, "I'm sorry, but this is not what I had in mind for my Friday; I would like to leave, please." The driver and pledge educators in charge of the activity ignore the pledge and refuse to let the pledge leave the vehicle; then, they start the car and drive away. The pledge educators are committing felonious restraint, a Class F Felony with a minimum of 13 to 16 months imprisonment. See Chapter Nineteen, Threats to Safety and Bodily Harm.

Involuntary Manslaughter

During pledging, the brothers of a fraternity "paddle" the pledges with wooden, frat-inscribed mini-canoe paddles that pledges receive when they accept their bids. After being hit by P with a paddle, one of the pledges, V, throws a blood clot and dies from a pulmonary embolism. P may be found guilty of involuntary manslaughter, a Class F Felony, in addition to hazing, a Class 2 Misdemeanor. See Chapter Twenty, Taking Another Person's Life and Chapter Twenty-Eight, Common Crimes Committed by Groups or During Group Initiations.

Felony Death by Vehicle

P is the sober team leader for a pledge scavenger hunt. The pledges are together in the backseat while P drives them from place to place, drinking at every stop. After the last stop, in haste to be the first team back to campus, P drives at an excessive *speed, loses control of the car, and crashes into a tree. One of the pledges, **V**, is thrown out of the car and dies from injuries suffered. **P** is guilty of felony death by vehicle, a Class E Felony.* **See Chapter Twenty-Seven, Other Driving Violations.**

Chapter 29
Crimes Against Children and Reporting Child Abuse

Contributing to Delinquency and Neglect of Minors

Over winter break, a college senior hosted a high school reunion party at her family's home and provided a keg of beer for her friends, all of whom were 21 years old and older. When the host's younger brother and his high school classmates, some of whom were under the age of 16, showed up at the house during the party, the host allowed them to have some of the beer. The host was arrested and charged with multiple counts of Contributing to Delinquency and Neglect of Minors – one count for each teenager under the age of 16 who was given alcohol. She was also charged with furnishing alcohol to persons under 21 years old and aiding and abetting the crime of possession and consumption of alcohol by persons under 21 years old.

Crime: The crime of contributing to delinquency of a minor and neglect by parents and others occurs when a person, at least 16 years old, knowingly or willfully causes, encourages, or aids any juvenile to be in a place or condition, or to commit an act for which the juvenile could be adjudicated delinquent, undisciplined, abused, or neglected.

The juvenile does not have to be found delinquent, undisciplined, abused, or neglected for the parent or other person at least 16 years old to be found guilty.

Type of Crime: Class 1 Misdemeanor

Punishment: Community punishment with up to 45 days in jail for failure to comply

Did You Know that anyone at least 16 years old can be guilty of contributing to delinquency and neglect of a minor?

Example: P is 18 years old, and P allows P's 15-year-old sister to drive P's car without a driver's license or learner's permit. P is guilty of contributing to delinquency and neglect of a minor.

Child Abuse

We have included this section to help you recognize if you have been a victim of child abuse, or if someone you know has been a victim of child abuse. In most instances, a person reports child abuse long after the abuse occurs. In fact, in many cases, the abuse occurs many times before the child tells anyone. We encourage you to report if you know anyone who is or has been abused.

Crime: The felony crime of child abuse occurs in any of the following situations:

- A parent or other person providing care to or supervision of a child less than 16 years old intentionally inflicts any serious physical injury upon or to the child or intentionally commits an assault upon the child that results in serious physical injury to the child;

- A parent of a child less than 16 years old, or any other person providing care to or supervision of the child, commits, permits, or encourages any act of prostitution with or by the child;

- A parent or legal guardian of a child less than 16 years old commits or allows the commission of any sexual act upon the child;

- A parent or any other person providing care to or supervision of a child less than 16 years old intentionally inflicts any serious bodily injury to the child or intentionally commits an assault upon the child that results in serious bodily injury to the child or that results in permanent or protracted loss or impairment of any mental or emotional function of the child; OR

- A parent or any other person providing care to or supervision of a child less than 16 years old, by a willful act or grossly negligent omission in the care of the child, shows a reckless disregard for human life, if the act or omission results in serious bodily or physical injury to the child.

Type of Crime: Class C Felony

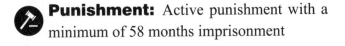 **Punishment:** Active punishment with a minimum of 58 months imprisonment

Example: *V, who is 14 years old, comes home later than V's curfew at home. V's father is angry and whips V with a belt until V has bruises, sores, and welts that last for over a week and that cause V to be unable to walk or sit for over a week. V's father is guilty of felony child abuse.*

Example: *P, a college student, is babysitting an infant. P becomes frustrated when the infant cries constantly and doesn't fall asleep. P shakes the infant until the baby becomes unconscious. The baby suffers brain damage. P is guilty of felony child abuse.*

Misdemeanor Child Abuse

Crime: The misdemeanor crime of child abuse occurs when any parent of a child less than 16 years old, or any other person providing care to or supervision of such child, inflicts physical injury, or allows physical injury to be inflicted, or creates or allows to be created a substantial risk of physical injury, upon or to such child by other than accidental means.

Type of Crime: Class A1 Misdemeanor

Punishment: Community, intermediate, or active punishment with up to 60 days in jail for active punishment or for failure to comply with community or intermediate punishment

Taking Indecent Liberties with a Child

Crime: The crime of taking indecent liberties with a child under the age of 16 years old occurs when a person 16 years old or older, and at least 5 years older than the child:

- Takes or attempts to take any immoral, improper or indecent liberties with any child for the purpose of arousing or gratifying sexual desire; OR

- Commits or attempts to commit any lewd or lascivious act upon or with the body or any body part of a child.

"Immoral, improper, or indecent liberties" is a broad term. The jury has wide discretion in determining what are "immoral, improper, or indecent liberties."

Taking indecent liberties with children does not require sexual intercourse or sodomy. The mere touching of a child for sexual gratification or to arouse the sexual desires of a child can be taking indecent liberties with children.

Taking indecent liberties with children does not require physical touching of a child. Masturbation in the presence of a child is taking indecent liberties with children.

Taking indecent liberties with children is gender-neutral. Males and females can be victims or perpetrators of taking indecent liberties with children.

Type of Crime: Class F Felony

Punishment: Intermediate or active punishment with a minimum of 13 months imprisonment for active punishment or for failure to comply with intermediate punishment

Example: *P is 18 years old, and V is 13 years old. P places P's hands on the breasts of V. P is guilty of taking indecent liberties with a child (felony), even if V consents to the touching.*

Dissemination to Minors Under 16 Years Old

Crime: A crime occurs when a person 18 years old or older knowingly disseminates to any minor under 16 years old material that the person knows or should reasonably know is obscene.

Type of Crime: Class I Felony

Punishment: Community punishment with a minimum of 4 months imprisonment for failure to comply

Example: *P, 18 years old, passes down his pornographic DVDs to his 15-year-old brother before he leaves for college. His brother brings them to a friend's house to show off and spend a Friday night in front of the high-def movies. The friend's parents find the boys watching the DVDs and ask where they got them. The* *boy tells the mother, who calls the police and reports **P**. **P** can be charged with a Class I Felony.*

Solicitation of Child by Computer to Commit an Unlawful Sex Act

Crime: The crime of solicitation of child by computer to commit an unlawful sex act occurs if a person, 16 years old or older, knowingly, with the intent to commit an unlawful sex act, entices, advises, coerces, orders, or commands – by means of a computer – a child who is less than 16 years old and at least 3 years younger than the person (or a person believed to be a child who is less than 16 years old and at least 3 years younger) to meet with the person or any other person for the purpose of committing an unlawful sex act.

Type of Crime: Class G Felony

Punishment: Intermediate or active punishment with a minimum of 10 months imprisonment for active punishment or failure to comply with intermediate punishment

Example: *P, 20 years old, posts a Craigslist®️ ad soliciting sexual contact with "sexy, young females." An undercover police officer responds to the ad with an e-mail claiming to be a 15-year-old female. P arranges for the two to meet at a local hotel to have sex. P is guilty*

of the felony crime of solicitation of child by computer to commit an unlawful sex act.

Reporting Child Abuse

North Carolina law requires that any person or institution who has cause to suspect that any juvenile is abused or neglected or has died as the result of maltreatment, shall report the case of that juvenile to the director of the department of social services in the county where the juvenile resides or is found. You may wonder if someone has the right to sue you if you report child abuse. The answer is no, if a report of child abuse is made in good faith.

A common question is whether a person should report child abuse if the person learns that a child was abused in the past, but is not currently being abused. The best answer is yes. There is no statute of limitations for prosecuting felonies in North Carolina. There is a two-year statute of limitations for prosecuting misdemeanors.

If you have been abused or know someone who has been abused, you can contact the Prevent Child Abuse North Carolina helpline toll-free at 1-800-CHILDREN (1-800-244-5373) or by e-mail at info@preventchildabusenc.org. All calls made to the Helpline are confidential.

Though reports of child abuse are confidential, if a criminal prosecution or lawsuit results from a report, the contents of the report may be disclosed, including the name of the person who made the report.

Chapter 30
Other Laws of Interest

Gambling

Texas Hold 'Em is vastly popular among adults and young people. Participating in NCAA basketball pools during March Madness is also popular. However, if the games are played for real money, then the participants are actually violating North Carolina law that prohibits playing a game of chance for money. Many people probably commit this crime without getting caught. However, the law is on the books, and just because other people do not get caught is not a guarantee that you will not be arrested.

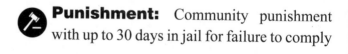 **Crime:** The crime of gambling occurs when a person plays at or bets on any game of chance at which any money, property, or other thing of value is bet.

Type of Crime: Class 2 Misdemeanor

Punishment: Community punishment with up to 30 days in jail for failure to comply

Example: *P and three of P's friends play a card game of Texas Hold 'Em, and they each buy poker chips to use in the game. All four persons are guilty of the crime of gambling.*

Pay Attention!
Even if you may not be criminally prosecuted for poker games or basketball pools, if you conduct these activities on school premises, you may be subject to punishment under school policies.

Littering

Crime: The crime of littering occurs when a person intentionally or recklessly throws, scatters, spills, or places litter upon any public property or private property not owned by the person.

Did You Know
that it is a crime to throw trash out of your car window?

Litter is defined as any garbage, rubbish, trash, refuse, can, bottle, box, container, wrapper, paper, paper product, tire, appliance, etc.

Type of Crime: Misdemeanor

Punishment: Fine of not less than $250, but not more than $1,000

Fire Alarms

Crime: A crime occurs when a person pulls a fire alarm, except in case of fire, or interferes with, misuses, or damages a fire alarm, fire detection, smoke detection, or fire extinguishing system.

Type of Crime: Class 2 Misdemeanor

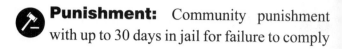

Punishment: Community punishment with up to 30 days in jail for failure to comply

Public Urination

Did You Know that it is a crime in most North Carolina cities to urinate in public view, even if urinating (openly) on private property?

In some local areas, including Chapel Hill and Charlotte-Mecklenburg, it is unlawful for any person to urinate or defecate on any public place, sidewalk, street, alleyway, right-of-way, or public building, or on private property.

Abortion

If you are least 18 years old, you can legally get an abortion without your parents' knowledge or consent. If you are under 18 years old, unmarried, and still under your parents' care and control, then an abortion may only proceed under very limited circumstances without your parents' consent.

Armed Services and Registration for the Draft

If you are 17 years old, you may join the military with the permission of a parent. If you are 18 years old, you may join the military without the consent of a parent.

Every male who is a United States citizen and most resident alien males must register for the draft when they turn 18 years old. You may receive a registration form in the mail, or you can find more information online.

X. Landlord/Tenant

Chapter 31
Landlord/Tenant

Chapter 31
Landlord/Tenant

Landlord/Tenant Issues

If you rent an apartment or house off-campus, you have experience with contracts and landlord/tenant law. The terms of the lease generally control the relationship between you and your landlord. Often the lease is a standard form, and you don't have much opportunity to negotiate it. However, there's a chance that you may be able to negotiate a provision or two, maybe in exchange for other terms. In any case, you need to read your lease carefully before you sign it. You don't want surprises later. Listed below are some questions you need to ask yourself as you review the lease. With answers to these questions, you will have a better understanding of your rights and responsibilities under the lease and hopefully avoid the unhappy consequences of violating the lease.

What am I leasing?

Make sure the description of the leased premises in the lease matches what you think you're leasing.

How long is my lease?

Usually one of the first paragraphs in the lease describes the term (or length) of the lease. Know the beginning date and the ending date of the lease. Sometimes, there is an initial term and then an automatic renewal of the term for some period (such as month-to-month). In other cases, there may be a right to renew the lease. If there is an automatic renewal provision, you need to pay attention to the notice provisions if you want to terminate the lease. If you have the right to renew the lease, make sure you know the deadline for giving notice of renewal and mark your calendar. Pay attention to the method of notice that is required by the lease (such as hand delivery, mail, or delivery service).

How much is the rent?

Look for the amount of the base monthly rent. Are there any additional rental amounts? Are there any rental increases after a certain time? If the lease has an automatic renewal clause, it may provide for an increase in rent, which will go into effect unless you give notice of termination. Be alert to any notice of rent increases that you receive during the lease, and, if you want to terminate the lease, provide any written notice of termination that is required by the lease on a timely basis. Pay attention to the method of notice that is required by the lease (such as hand delivery, mail, or delivery service).

When is my rent due?

Rent is due on or before the due date. If rent is due on the first of the month, you will need to be sure to send it ahead of time so that it arrives by the first of the month. Pay attention to any late fees that may be due if your payment is late. Under North Carolina law, late fees cannot exceed $15 or 5% of monthly rent, whichever is greater, if rent is paid monthly. Late fees cannot be charged until the payment is late by 5 or more days. Avoid this extra expense by marking your calendar and paying on time. Leases also sometimes include a "returned check" fee if your check is returned for insufficient funds. To avoid this fee, be sure your bank account has a sufficient balance to cover the rent check until it clears the bank.

Where do I pay my rent?

Most leases specify to whom to make your payment and an address to send your payment. If you have a roommate, check to see if the landlord will accept multiple payments or require one payment. If you pay in cash, be sure to get a receipt.

What if my roommate doesn't pay her share of the rent or damages the property?

If you have a roommate, check for a **joint and several liability** clause. This means that *you* are responsible if your roommate doesn't pay her share of the rent or breaches the lease in any other way. And it works the other way around, too.

Example: *Your roommate drops out of school due to poor grades and moves out of the apartment. Your roommate had done a bit of partying during the semester, which had resulted in a hole in the wall and broken window. Your roommate does not repair these damages. Your roommate also does not pay for one-half of the remaining rent. If the lease contains a joint and several liability clause, you will be responsible to pay the remaining rent as well as the cost to repair the damages.*

Is a security deposit or other deposit required?

Landlords often require a security deposit, particularly when renting to students. In North Carolina, the maximum amount a landlord can charge for a security deposit is 1.5 months for a month-to-month lease and 2 months for a yearly lease. You usually cannot apply the security deposit to your rent during the term of the lease, but your landlord may allow you to apply it to your last month's rent. The landlord has the right to use the security deposit to cover money owed by you or damages or repairs beyond "normal wear and tear," but otherwise must return the balance to you within 30 days after the end of your lease and provide a written account to you of any amount withheld. Be sure you leave a forwarding address with the landlord so you will receive a check for the balance. If you have a pet, be sure the lease has a provision allowing pets. The landlord may also require a pet deposit, which is usually nonrefundable.

Do I pay for utilities?

Check closely to see if you will need to pay for utilities in addition to rent. Sometimes landlords will pay for a portion of the utilities (like water and sewer) and require you to pay the electrical and gas bills. In buildings with multiple units, gas and electric are often separately metered for each unit, and water is metered for the whole building. In this case, you need to be sure that water will not be charged separately to you. You also need to ask whether common areas have a separate meter and be sure that you will not be charged for utilities in common areas on your utility bills (such as hall or exterior lights or washer/dryer appliances). You may need to set up an account with a utility company and pay a deposit to obtain service.

Do I have to obtain insurance?

Check your lease to see if it requires you to provide either liability or contents insurance. In any case, it's a good idea for you to have contents insurance on your own furniture and belongings. Check to see if your insurance covers both destruction and theft. The landlord will usually have insurance on the land and building the landlord owns, but the landlord's insurance will not cover or replace your possessions if they are destroyed. The lease may also require you to indemnify (or reimburse) the landlord if the landlord incurs any damages or expenses resulting from harm to your guests or your property.

Can I terminate my lease early?

Many leases do not allow you to terminate your lease until the end of a term or a renewal period. Even if you are allowed to break your lease, there is usually a requirement that you pay rent until the landlord finds another tenant or until the end of the lease, whichever is the shorter period. Most leases will require you to give advance written notice of any termination. Pay attention to the notice requirements (including the method of delivery), and mark your calendar. If your landlord makes an oral promise to you that you can move out early without financial consequences, be sure to get this promise in writing.

Can I sublease or assign my lease?

Most leases require you to obtain the written consent of the landlord in order to sublease or assign it. Some leases prohibit any sublease or assignment. Check this provision carefully if you have any intention of subleasing or assigning your lease (for instance, if you plan to sublease your apartment during the summer).

❗ Pay Attention!

Subletting without your landlord's consent (if required) is a misdemeanor in North Carolina.

What are the repair obligations of the landlord? What are my repair obligations?

Landlords are required to provide you with a habitable residence. In North Carolina, that means your electrical, plumbing, sanitary, heating, ventilating, air conditioning, and other facilities and appliances supplied by the landlord are in good and safe working order. Under most leases, landlords have the primary maintenance responsibility for these items. You generally have the responsibility to keep the premises clean and to use the appliances and equipment properly. You may have light maintenance responsibilities, such as replacing light bulbs and heating and air conditioning filters. If you see something that your landlord needs to repair (like a leaky pipe), you need to report it to your landlord immediately, even if it's not convenient for you to take the time to notify your landlord. Put your request in writing! The reason immediate notice is important is because you have a duty to "mitigate damages." If you fail to report a problem (like a leaky pipe) until it becomes a major crisis (like rotting wood and mold from water damage), you could be held responsible for the additional damages caused by your delay in reporting.

If the premises become uninhabitable, you may have the right to move out or to receive a reduction in your rent for the period of time that the premises are uninhabitable. In this case, you will need to seek legal advice to determine your options.

Can the landlord enter the premises at any time?

Generally, the landlord has the right to enter the premises at reasonable times to conduct inspections or maintenance, to make improvements, and to ensure health and safety. You shouldn't expect to see your landlord barging into your apartment or home for no apparent reason.

In what condition do I have to return the property?

Your lease will either require you to return the premises in "good condition" or in "at least the same condition as it was at the beginning of the lease," in either case usually excluding ordinary wear and tear. To protect yourself, you should take pictures of the property before you move in, e-mail the pictures to yourself, and save the e-mail as documented proof of the condition of the property at the beginning of the lease. You should follow the same procedure at the end of the lease. If possible, suggest that you and the landlord conduct a walkthrough of the property at the beginning and at the end of the lease to determine if there are any items that need repair. The lease may also require an inspection of the premises. Taking these steps will help you get back as much of your security deposit as you are entitled.

If you are subletting an apartment or house, you may be responsible for any damage caused by the previous tenant, unless you work something else out with the landlord.

Do I have a right to make improvements or alterations to the apartment or house (such as attaching shelving to the wall, painting, putting up a wall, etc.)? If so, do I have to remove the improvements at the end of the lease?

Leases generally require you to obtain the written permission of the landlord before making any improvements or alterations to an apartment or house. The improvements or alterations will usually become the property of the landlord unless the landlord otherwise agrees in writing. If you plan to make some changes that you want to take with you at the end of the lease, you need to be sure to get the landlord to agree to this arrangement in writing. On the other hand, some leases may require you to remove any improvements or alterations and repair any damages caused by the improvements or alterations.

Will I have any responsibility for damages to common areas not caused by me?

If you are in a building with multiple units and common areas (like hallways, lobbies, lounges, laundry room, exercise room, pools, game rooms, etc.), check your lease or ask your landlord to see if you will have any responsibility for damages to common areas that are not caused by you.

Are there any special rules and restrictions?

Leases often spell out rules about such issues as firearms, drugs, criminal conduct, noise, garbage, and outdoor cooking, among other rules. The landlord may also have written rules and regulations in addition to the lease and assess fines for violation of rules. Pay attention to these rules not only for yourself but as they apply to any guests that you may have on the premises.

What is a default under my lease?

Leases generally provide that you will be in default if you fail to pay rent, vacate the premises before the end of the lease, fail to maintain the premises, conduct illegal activities (like drugs or underage drinking), sublet the premises without the landlord's permission, have pets if pets are prohibited, or breach any provision of the lease. The consequences of default can be severe, so it's important to be familiar with the provisions of the lease and what constitutes a default.

Can I stop my rent payments if my landlord breaches the lease?

If your landlord breaches the lease (for example, doesn't maintain the air conditioning properly), you are *not* entitled to breach the lease, too, by not paying rent. One breach does not justify another breach under landlord/tenant law. However, if your landlord doesn't respond, you could arrange for the repairs yourself and deduct the cost from your rent payment. You will need to save any bills documenting your expenses.

Do I have a grace period to correct a default under my lease?

Check your lease to see if you have a right to notice of a default from the landlord and an opportunity to cure it before the landlord declares you in default. Some leases call for instant default without any right of notice if you breach the lease. Compliance with the provisions of a lease is not something to take lightly. And just because your landlord gives you a "pass" on one violation doesn't mean that the landlord will give you a second chance or that you're entitled to another "pass." In fact, most leases specifically state that a waiver of one breach doesn't constitute a waiver of all future breaches.

What rights does the landlord have if I default?

Leases often provide that landlords can terminate your right to possession, terminate the lease, accelerate your rent payments, and/or evict you if you default under the lease. Pay attention to the terms and conditions of eviction in your lease.

Do I have any rights if others are disturbing my enjoyment of the premises?

Leases often provide that a tenant has a right of "quiet enjoyment." This means that if you pay all amounts owed and perform all obligations under the lease, you may peacefully and quietly enjoy the premises.

What can I do if I have a dispute with the landlord?

Of course, first try to resolve the dispute with your landlord without taking any legal action. If these efforts are not successful, your lease may have a dispute resolution provision. Some may require arbitration or mediation; others may specify the court where lawsuits must be brought. Under some leases, you may waive your right to a jury trial. Be familiar with any dispute resolution provisions before the dispute arises. Unless the lease provides otherwise, small claims courts often hear cases involving landlord/tenant issues.

Glossary

Definition of Certain Legal Terms as Used in This Book

Accessory: a person who aids or contributes in the commission or concealment of a crime

Active Punishment: punishment that requires incarceration in the state prison system

Aid and Abet: to assist or facilitate the commission of a crime or to promote its accomplishment

Arrest: the taking of a person into custody against the person's will for the purpose of criminal prosecution or interrogation

Civil law: the body of law that defines the rights and obligations between private citizens, such as contract law or tort law

Community Punishment: punishment that does not involve prison, jail, or an intermediate punishment, but instead may include fines, restitution, community service, and/or substance abuse treatment

Consent: agreement, approval, or permission as to some act or purpose

Crime: an act of doing something that violates written law or the failure to do something required by law that may be punished by the state

Criminal law: body of law that defines crimes and the punishments for violating them

Custody: detention of a person in a situation in which a person is under arrest or a reasonable person does not feel free to leave

Defendant: a person who is charged with committing a crime; also called offender or perpetrator

District Attorney: the elected attorney who oversees the prosecution of crimes

District Court: the court in North Carolina that has jurisdiction over misdemeanors

Expunction: the act of having a criminal conviction erased from an individual's record

Felon: a person convicted of a felony

Felony: crime for which the punishment is imprisonment in the State's prison system, life imprisonment, or death

Fine: money required to be paid as punishment for violation of a law or ordinance

Frisk: pat-down of outer clothing performed by a police officer if the police officer has a reasonable suspicion that criminal activity has just taken place or is about to take place and reason to believe that a person is armed and dangerous

Guilt Beyond a Reasonable Doubt: standard of proof that a prosecutor must satisfy to prove a person committed a crime

Imprisonment: sentence given to a person convicted of a crime to be served in a prison or jail; also called incarceration

Incarceration: sentence given to a person convicted of a crime to be served in a prison or jail; also called imprisonment

Intermediate Punishment: punishment that is supervised probation with one or more of the following: split sentencing (jail time plus community options), electronic house arrest, intensive supervision, a residential center, a day reporting center, or a drug treatment center

Juvenile: generally, a person under 16 years old in North Carolina

Minor: a person who has not yet reached legal age; in North Carolina, a person reaches legal age at 16, 18, or 21 years old, based on the circumstances

Miranda Warnings: cautionary instructions that law enforcement must give a person in custody before interrogation

Misdemeanant: a person convicted of a misdemeanor

Misdemeanor: any crime that is not a felony

Offender: a person who is charged with committing a crime or violation of law; also called defendant or perpetrator

Ordinance: law passed by the governing authority of a city or county

Parole: early release from prison

Parties to a Crime: all persons involved in committing, planning, participating, helping, advising, encouraging, or benefiting in a criminal activity

Perpetrator: a person who is charged with committing a crime or violation of law; also called defendant or offender

Plain View Doctrine: doctrine that allows a police officer to seize without a search warrant evidence of a crime that is in plain view during a lawful observation

Probable Cause: the belief of a reasonable person that a crime has been committed or that evidence of a crime is at a particular location; probable cause is more than reasonable suspicion, but less than proof of guilt beyond a reasonable doubt

Probation: punishment for a violation of law served outside of prison with certain conditions, restrictions, and requirements

Prosecution: the process of charging and proving that a person committed a crime beyond a reasonable doubt

Prosecutor: the person who handles the prosecution of a crime against a defendant

Proximate Cause: an act or omission that directly causes something to occur

Reasonable Suspicion: belief of a reasonable person that is based on more than a hunch but less than probable cause that criminal activity has just taken place or is about to take place

Restitution: monetary reimbursement

Search Warrant: document obtained by a law enforcement official upon proof to a judge of probable cause to conduct a search of a person or property

Self-incrimination: the act of saying or doing something that will cause a person to appear guilty of a crime

Sentence: punishment issued by a judge (or jury in a death penalty case) to a person who is guilty of committing a crime

Sentencing Guidelines: guidelines with which North Carolina judges must comply when sentencing convicted offenders

Serious Bodily Injury: injury that causes a coma or permanent damage to a body part or organ

Serious Injury: physical injury that causes great pain and suffering

Sexual Act: oral act, anal sex, and any penetration other than vaginal intercourse, however slight, by any object into the genital or anal opening of another person's body

Sexual Intercourse: vaginal intercourse

State Action Doctrine: legal doctrine that provides that the United States Constitution only applies to governmental entities

State Legislature: the governing body of North Carolina consisting of two bodies (the House of Representatives and the Senate) elected by the people that enacts written laws

Statute: written law enacted by the state legislature that is included in The General Statutes of North Carolina

Statute of Limitations: time limit or deadline imposed by law regulating when a civil lawsuit must be filed or a criminal prosecution must be started

Summons: an order for a person to appear in court on a specific date and at a specific time

Superior Court: the court in North Carolina that has jurisdiction over felonies

The General Statutes of North Carolina: the complete set of statutes enacted by the state legislature in North Carolina

United States Constitution: the supreme law of the United States, which includes Amendments, such as the First, Fourth, Fifth, and Sixth Amendments

United States Supreme Court: the highest court in the United States which reviews cases decided by other courts and interprets questions about the United States Constitution

Victim: a person against whom a crime is committed

Index Topics

Note: Unitalicized numbers reference text; italicized numbers reference examples.

Appendix

Citations of Statutes

I. Starting College

II. The System

Chapter 5: Going to Trial and Getting Sentenced
  Citizens Guide to Structured Sentencing: *http://www.nccourts.org/Courts/*
  CRS/Councils/spac/Documents/citizenguide2008.pdf

III. Search, Arrest, and Speech: Your Rights Under the Constitution

Chapter 6: Your Constitutional Rights: Search and Seizure
  General authorization; definition of *consent*: N.C. Gen. Stat. § 15A-221
  Other searches and seizures: N.C. Gen. Stat. § 15A-231

Chapter 7: Your Constitutional Rights: Arrests
  Arrest by law enforcement officer: N.C. Gen. Stat. § 15A-401

IV. Substances: Alcohol, Drugs, and Driving

Chapter 9: Alcohol and Underage Drinking
  Sale to or purchase by underage persons: N.C. Gen. Stat. § 18B-302
  Penalties for certain offenses related to underage persons: N.C. Gen. Stat.
  § 18B-302.1
  Revocation for underage purchasers of alcohol: N.C. Gen. Stat. § 20-17.3
  Exemptions: N.C. Gen. Stat. § 18B-103
  Claim for relief created for sale to underage person: N.C. Gen. Stat. §
  18B-121
  Common-law rights not abridged: N.C. Gen. Stat. § 18B-128
  Youth employment: N.C. Gen. Stat. § 95-25.5
  Intoxicated and Disruptive in Public: N.C. Gen. Stat. § 14-444
  Blood Alcohol Percentage Charts:
  http://pubs.niaaa.nih.gov/publications/niaaa-guide/descFig7.htm

Chapter 10: Fake Identification and Misrepresentation of Age
  Possession or manufacture of certain fraudulent forms of identification:
  N.C. Gen. Stat. § 14-100.1

Violations of license or learner's permit provisions: N.C. GEN. STAT. § 20-30

Sale to or purchase by underage persons: N.C. GEN. STAT. § 18B-302

Identity theft: N.C. GEN. STAT. § 14-113.20

Chapter 11: Possession and Sale of Legal and Illegal Drugs

Violations; penalties: N.C. GEN. STAT. § 90-95

Schedule I controlled substances: N.C. GEN. STAT. § 90-89

Schedule II controlled substances: N.C. GEN. STAT. § 90-90

Schedule III controlled substances: N.C. GEN. STAT. § 90-91

Schedule IV controlled substances: N.C. GEN. STAT. § 90-92

Schedule V controlled substances: N.C. GEN. STAT. § 90-93

Schedule VI controlled substances: N.C. GEN. STAT. § 90-94

Student Aid Eligibility Worksheet for FAFSA – Drug Conviction: *http://www.fafsa.ed.gov/before013.htm*

Chapter 12: Possession and Sale of Marijuana

Violations; penalties: N.C. GEN. STAT. § 90-95

Schedule VI controlled substances: N.C. GEN. STAT. § 90-94

Chapter 13: Other Drug-Related Laws

Violations; penalties: N.C. GEN. STAT. § 90-95

Employing or intentionally using minor to commit a drug law violation: N.C. GEN. STAT. § 90-95.4

Inhaling fumes for purpose of causing intoxication: N.C. GEN. STAT. § 90-113.10

Possession of drug paraphernalia: N.C. GEN. STAT. § 90-113.22

Chapter 14: Drinking, Drugs, and Driving

Driving by person less than 21 years old after consuming alcohol or drugs: N.C. GEN. STAT. § 20-138.3

Implied consent to chemical analysis; mandatory revocation of license in event of refusal; right of driver to request analysis: N.C. GEN. STAT. § 20-16.2

Transporting an open container of alcoholic beverage: N.C. GEN. STAT. §
20-138.7

Manner of transportation: N.C. GEN. STAT. § 18B-401

Sentencing hearing after conviction for impaired driving; determination of
grossly aggravating and aggravating and mitigating factors; punishments:
N.C. GEN. STAT. § 20-179

V. Sex and Sexual Exploitation

Chapter 15: Sex Crimes with Force
  Second-degree rape: N.C. GEN. STAT. § 14-27.3
  First-degree rape: N.C. GEN. STAT. § 14-27.2
  Contaminate food or drink to render one mentally incapacitated or
  physically helpless: N.C. GEN. STAT. § 14-401.16
  First-degree sexual offense: N.C. GEN. STAT. § 14-27.4
  Second-degree sexual offense: N.C. GEN. STAT. § 14-27.5
  Sexual battery: N.C. GEN. STAT. § 14-27.5A
  Sex Offender Registry: *http://ncdoj.gov/Protect-Yourself/Find-Sex-*
  Offenders/SexOffenderRegPrograms.aspx

Chapter 16: Sexting and Sexual Exploitation of Minors
  First-degree sexual exploitation of a minor: N.C. GEN. STAT. § 14-190.16
  Second-degree sexual exploitation of a minor: N.C. GEN. STAT. § 14-
  190.17
  Third-degree sexual exploitation of a minor: N.C. GEN. STAT. § 14-
  190.17A

Chapter 17: Age of Consent and Statutory Rape
  Statutory rape or sexual offense of person who is 13, 14, or 15 years old:
  N.C. GEN. STAT. § 14-27.7A

Chapter 18: Other Sex Crimes
  Indecent exposure: N.C. GEN. STAT. § 14-190.9

Secretly peeping into room occupied by another person: N.C. GEN. STAT. § 14-202

VI. Safety and Injury: Threats and Bodily Harm to You and Others

Chapter 19: Threats to Safety and Bodily Harm
Misdemeanor assaults, batteries, and affrays, simple and aggravated; punishments: N.C. GEN. STAT. § 14-33
Assault inflicting serious bodily injury; strangulation; penalties: N.C. GEN. STAT. § 14-32.4
Felonious assault with deadly weapon with intent to kill or inflicting serious injury; punishments: N.C. GEN. STAT. § 14-32
Resisting officers: N.C. GEN. STAT. § 14-223
Communicating threats: N.C. GEN. STAT. § 14-277.1
Stalking: N.C. GEN. STAT. § 14-277.3A
Cyberstalking: N.C. GEN. STAT. § 14-196.3
Felonious restraint: N.C. GEN. STAT. § 14-43.3

Chapter 20: Taking Another Person's Life
Murder in the first and second degree defined; punishment: N.C. GEN. STAT. § 14-17
Punishment for manslaughter: N.C. GEN. STAT. § 14-18

Chapter 22: Weapons and Firearms
Weapons on campus or other educational property: N.C. GEN. STAT. § 14-269.2
Selling or giving weapons to minors: N.C. GEN. STAT. § 14-315
Carrying concealed weapons: N.C. GEN. STAT. § 14-269

VII. Property: Your Property and the Property of Others

Chapter 23: Stealing

Larceny from a merchant: N.C. GEN. STAT. § 14-72.11

Concealment of merchandise in mercantile establishments: N.C. GEN. STAT. § 14-72.1

Distinctions between grand and petit larceny abolished; punishment; accessories to larceny: N.C. GEN. STAT. § 14-70

Receiving stolen goods; receiving or possessing goods represented as stolen: N.C. GEN. STAT. § 14-71

Larceny of property; receiving stolen goods or possessing stolen goods: N.C. GEN. STAT. § 14-72

Petty misdemeanors: N.C. GEN. STAT. § 14-73.1

Larceny by servants and other employees: N.C. GEN. STAT. § 14-74

Civil liability for larceny, shoplifting, theft by employee, embezzlement, and obtaining property by false pretense: N.C. GEN. STAT. § 1-538.2

Chapter 24: Invading Another Person's Property

First-degree trespass: N.C. GEN. STAT. § 14-159.12

Second-degree trespass: N.C. GEN. STAT. § 14-159.13

Willful and wanton injury to real property: N.C. GEN. STAT. § 14-127

Willful and wanton injury to personal property: N.C. GEN. STAT. § 14-160

First- and second-degree burglary: N.C. GEN. STAT. § 14-51

Breaking or entering buildings generally: N.C. GEN. STAT. § 14-54

Breaking or entering a building that is a place of religious worship: N.C. GEN. STAT. § 14-54.1

Breaking or entering into or breaking out of railroad cars, motor vehicles, trailers, aircraft, boats, or other watercraft: N.C. GEN. STAT. § 14-56

Chapter 25: Intellectual Property and Electronic Crimes

Piracy: *http://www.riaa.com, http://www.fbi.gov/ipr/*

Computer trespass: N.C. GEN. STAT. § 14-458

VIII. Staying the Course: Driving, Driving Violations, and Accidents

Chapter 26: What to Do if You Are Pulled Over or in an Accident
Duty to stop in event of a crash; furnishing information or assistance to injured person, etc.; persons assisting exempt from civil liability: N.C. GEN. STAT. § 20-166

Chapter 27: Other Driving Violations
Felony and misdemeanor death by vehicle; felony serious injury by vehicle; aggravated offenses; repeat felony death by vehicle: N.C. GEN. STAT. § 20-141.4
Reckless driving: N.C. GEN. STAT. § 20-140
Unlawful racing on streets and highways: N.C. GEN. STAT. § 20-141.3
Aggressive Driving: N.C. GEN. STAT. § 20-141.6
Duty to stop in event of a crash; furnishing information or assistance to injured person, etc.; persons assisting exempt from civil liability: N.C. GEN. STAT. § 20-166
Reports and investigations required in event of accident: N.C. GEN. STAT. § 20-166.1
Unlawful to permit unlicensed minor to drive motor vehicle: N.C. GEN. STAT. § 20-32
Authority of Division to suspend license: N.C. GEN. STAT. § 20-16
Mandatory revocation of license by Division: N.C. GEN. STAT. § 20-17
North Carolina Department of Motor Vehicles: *http://www.ncdot.org/dmv/*
North Carolina Driver's Handbook: *http://www.ncdot.org/dmv/driver_services/drivershandbook/*

IX. Other Criminal Laws and Topics of Interest: Groups and Group Initiations, Crimes Against Children, and More

Chapter 28: Common Crimes Committed by Groups or During Group Initiations

Hazing: N.C. GEN. STAT. § 14-35

Chapter 29: Crimes Against Children & Reporting Child Abuse
Contributing to delinquency and neglect by parents and others: N.C. GEN. STAT. § 14-316.1
Child abuse a felony: N.C. GEN. STAT. § 14-318.4
Child abuse a Class 1 [A1] misdemeanor: N.C. Gen. Stat. § 14-318.2
Duty to report abuse, neglect, dependency, or death due to maltreatment: N.C. GEN. STAT. § 7B-301
Taking indecent liberties with children: N.C. GEN. STAT. § 14-202.1
Solicitation of child by computer to commit an unlawful sex act: N.C. GEN. STAT. § 14-202.3
Dissemination to minors under the age of 16 years: N.C. GEN. STAT. § 14-190.7

Chapter 30: Other Laws of Interest
Gambling: N.C. GEN. STAT. § 14-292
Littering: N.C. GEN. STAT. § 14-399
Giving false fire alarms: N.C. GEN. STAT. § 14-286

About the Authors

 J.Tom Morgan is a nationally recognized expert on the prosecution of crimes against children and has appeared on CNN, the Oprah Winfrey Show, Court TV, the Today Show, and 48 Hours. He served as the District Attorney of DeKalb County for twelve years and was one of the first prosecutors in the country to specialize in the prosecution of crimes against children. Among his numerous awards, J.Tom was the first United States prosecutor to receive the Special Achievement Award from the International Association of Prosecutors. J.Tom has dedicated his career to child advocacy and is committed to helping young people avoid being both victims and perpetrators of crimes. Currently, he is a trial lawyer in private practice in Decatur, Georgia, specializing in criminal and civil litigation.

 Wilson Parker is a professor at Wake Forest University School of Law. He is an expert teacher and scholar in the area of Constitutional Law. Prior to joining the faculty, Wilson was a trial lawyer in private practice in North Carolina, litigating employment, civil rights, and civil liberties cases. He is a primary author, with Michael Curtis, of *Constitutional Law in Context*, a Constitutional Law casebook that is in its third edition. Wilson served as Chairman of the Amicus Curiae Committee of the North Carolina Advocates for Justice for several years and served on the Board of the North Carolina Center for Death Penalty Litigation.

To Order This Book

Online

Purchase at www.ignoranceisnodefense.com or www.amazon.com

Purchase Orders

Send or FAX your purchase order to:

Westchester Legal Press, LLC
P.O. Box 1324
Decatur, GA 30031

E-mail: info@ignoranceisnodefense.com

FAX: (404) 373-6418

Phone

Call: (404) 373-6453

For Speaking Engagements

Contact J.Tom Morgan or Wilson Parker at
info@ignoranceisnodefense.com

www.ignoranceisnodefense.com